?en Door on Mark

Open Door on Mark

His Gospel Explored

Phillip McFadyen

TRIANGLE

First Published in Great Britain in 1997
Triangle
SPCK Holy Trinity Church
Marylebone Road
London NW1 4DU

Bible passages and quotations are from the *New International Version* © 1973, 1978, 1984 by the International Bible Society, Published by Hodder & Stoughton.

British Library Cataloguing-in-Publication Data
A catalogue record of this book is available from the British Library

ISBN 0-281-04998-X

Typeset by David Benham, Norwich
Printed in Great Britain by Arrowsmiths Ltd, Bristol

Contents

Foreword

If we want to love God totally, the way forward is through prayer. We must learn (as prayer makes possible) to see the beauty of God in all that we experience in our day – and we must read his Word, the Scriptures.

Reading the Scriptures is not an easy matter. Truly to understand demands attention, time and meditation. We must first grasp what these authors, so very far away from us in time, meant to express, literally. Then we must understand what they meant, spiritually. And then we must pray this knowledge into personal life within us.

What Phillip McFadyen does for us is to share his own meditation. He has read and reread every passage, using the tools of biblical scholarship, and then, bringing to bear his own faith, his own desire to come close to God. This treasure he offers us, for our own use. Notice this book is not merely to be 'read'. It has to be savoured intimately, lived, prayed; just as the author did when writing it. It challenges our earnestness as Christians, and gives us the material to deepen our love for our Lord. There is nothing more precious. We owe Phillip McFadyen a deep debt of gratitude. Perhaps we could repay him in prayer?

Sister Wendy Beckett

Preface

'I stand at the door and knock' (Rev. 3.20) is the subtext behind Holman Hunt's famous painting *The Light of the World*. Sadly this may be said of many who approach the Bible. It is a closed book to them. In the painting, the ivy-clad door stands barred to the disconsolate figure. There is little optimism that entry might be gained. All there is left to do is to stand at the door and knock.

The situation today reminds me of the time when Bibles were chained or written in Latin. Access was limited to the privileged few, the devout and the initiated. Currently Scripture is widely available but largely unread. Less than 30 per cent of churchgoers read their Bible and those who do not attend church find the Scriptures unintelligible. A closed mind attitude prevails, both among churchgoers and those on the outside looking in. What is needed now is a new look at Scripture which frees it from preconceptions – a simple but challenging approach which helps ordinary people 'hear Jesus gladly' as they did in Mark's time when Jesus 'taught them as one who had authority, not as the teachers of the law' (1.22).

Those who are intrigued by the figure of Jesus are often put off by the Church. Indeed to cross the threshold of a church door requires courage and determination. Often the door is physically barred with no help as to where to find the key. Sadly, fear of vandalism and exposure has driven the Church into a ghetto for the initiated. Those seeking are locked out with little to help them gain entry.

Even the Gospels themselves have become subjected to a 'lock up' mentality. Commentaries abound but they are usually one of two types: either the devotional aid or the theological treatise. Those that claim to be a simple introduction treat their readers as if they were simple and unquestioning. This little book claims only to open a door for those genuinely wanting to discuss the good news as Mark saw it.

Mark, of all the Gospel writers, is direct, racy, forceful and breathless in his presentation. It is written with an urgency which sweeps the reader along. He has no time to discuss details of biography – how

Jesus was born, what he looked like, whether he was married, kosher, or rabbinically trained. Mark writes for those intrigued by the questions 'Who is Jesus?' 'What does he stand for?' This Gospel is meant to confront us with the challenge of discipleship and it talks of a kingdom achieved through death and glory.

This little guide attempts to nudge the door open for those with questions to ask. There are suggestions as to how the book might be used in groups and as an opener for discussion.

My thanks to all those who have encouraged me to produce these notes especially the people of St Helen's, Ranworth, who have engaged in a study of Mark with me over the last three years. Their 'open-door policy' to the hundred thousand visitors we receive annually has been an inspiration to this theme of an open door. I would also like to thank the Rt. Revd Peter Nott who first suggested this sort of commentary for use in the diocese of Norwich, Hubert Richards with whom I have had the privilege to teach for many years and who assiduously checked the proofs. My thanks to David Benham who dealt with the typescript and to my wife and family for their patience and encouragement. Finally I owe a debt of gratitude to my former tutor, Professor Morna Hooker, who taught me most of what I know about Mark's Gospel and who kindly looked over my text prior to publication. Her definitive commentary *The Gospel According to St Mark*, A. & C. Black, 1991, is the rock from which these notes are hewn.

Phillip McFadyen

How to use this book

For many people the thought of Bible study is a non-starter. They often think that

* it is for the pious.
* they need to leave their brains outside.
* they have to be solemn and sanctimonious.

None of this is necessary, especially when studying Mark's Gospel. Remember, the Jesus of this Gospel is urgent, direct and even confrontational. He is not comfortable with the pious and loses his temper with his own disciples when they are wooden-headed and difficult.

Engaging with this Gospel is challenging, even threatening. We cannot be complacent when reading it.

So Bible study is not for the timid or those of a nervous disposition. What you are about to engage in is exciting and may even change your life.

This book is less of a commentary and more of a discussion starter – it is meant to probe rather than provide answers.

There are a number of ways to use the book:

1) It falls neatly into ten sections so it can provide a ten-week course of weekday studies.
2) It can also be used in conjunction with Advent and Lent study groups. Sections 1–4 can be used during the four weeks of Advent. (This will take a group up to the Markan watershed in chapter 8.) Sections 6–10 can be used during the six weeks of Lent. (This will take the group up to the resurrection at Easter.)
3) It can be used for private Bible study and read through continuously at one sitting. (This may be dangerous. Anthony Bloom, as a young agnostic, found himself being converted by reading Mark at one

sitting – he is now a metropolitan archbishop of the Russian Orthodox Church!)

Working with a Group

This book is designed to be used in groups. It is meant to encourage discussion and debate. If you engage in this method you need to have some clear aims.

First, stick to the text of Mark. People are easily diverted into general discussion about the state of the Church and about morality and are even happy to give their prejudices an airing. Mark's Gospel is the perfect antidote to this. Jesus, in this Gospel, is single-minded and we should be also.

Give everyone a chance to participate. Look for the naturally reticent and invite them to comment or tell their story. Remember how Jesus does this with the woman with the issue of blood (5.25–34). Such people often have the brightest pearls but their shell needs opening.

It will help to keep your group focused by having some clear questions to set before them. Have some answers in mind but try to encourage them to formulate their own response. For instance:

A) Why was Mark written?
   In answer to the questions: 'Who is Jesus?' 'What does he stand for?'
B) For whom was this Gospel written?
   For those who want to follow Jesus – his disciples.
C) What does the Gospel of Mark say?
   In order to be a disciple you need to follow Jesus through suffering to glory.

Ice-breakers

Openness is the theme: being open to the good news as Mark presents it, being open to one another as we discover what discipleship means. To achieve this, it might help to arrange for your group to get to know each other better. This will enable them to participate more fully. If Bible study is to be fun and enjoyable then you want everyone to get involved as soon as possible. Here are some suggestions.

1) Listening Exercise. Number the members of the group one-two-three, one-two-three, one-two-three. Ask 'number ones' to tell 'number twos' who they are, where they are from and what they enjoy doing. 'Number two' then introduces 'number one' to 'number three' and they then compare notes. This is a good exercise in listening, especially for the 'number twos'.
2) Buzz groups. Divide the group into threes and compile a list of favourite stories from Mark. This will encourage familiarity with the Gospel and whet appetites for the study.

These exercises are not necessary but might encourage your group to gel if they do not know each other. They should take no more than ten minutes at the most.

How to Organize the Bible Study

First you need to decide how long you have and how much ground you intend to cover.

Studying One Section

First, set aside an hour to familiarize the group with a whole section, for example, section 7, 'Open to the Challenge'.

- Arrange your group in a circle.
- Allocate twelve minutes for each 'day reading'. (There are five to each section.)
- Invite members to read aloud, in turn, through the first reading, for example, 'Sabbath Conflicts', Mark 2.23—3.12 (section 2, reading 6). This should take two to three minutes.
- The leader then either reads out the commentary or summarizes it.
- Divide the people into 'buzz groups' of three members each and ask them to consider one of the questions listed in connection with the passage.
- Stop the discussion after five minutes.
- Repeat this procedure for the remaining four readings of the section.

If you keep to the suggested timing, this should take only one hour and will stimulate your group to study Mark's Gospel further. The whole process will be facilitated by asking your group to read through the material before the meeting.

If this is a successful procedure, and your group wants to do more, you might arrange a monthly ongoing Bible study to cover the whole Gospel in ten months, or ten weeks if you meet weekly.

Studying One Reading

This will look at one reading of the section in more detail, for example, 'The Parable about Rejection', Mark 12.1–12 (section 7, reading 33). Again, allow at least one hour for this exercise.

• Arrange seating in a circle.
• Emphasize the context by referring to the section title, 'Open to the Challenge'. This will help the group understand Mark's theme better.
• Invite members to read the text out loud in turn.
• The leader reads out the commentary and invites others to make their observations. Do they agree, or disagree? Are they challenged? Have they anything they want to add? What does the passage say to them about openness? How does it apply to their church situations?
• Divide the people into smaller groups to tackle the set questions, perhaps allocating different questions to different groups, or all tackling the questions together, depending upon the time available.
• Draw together the discussion by inviting comments and insights to be shared in the final plenary session.

Obviously this method is going to be more demanding on time, especially if the group if committed to an ongoing study of the whole Gospel. This needs to be discussed with the group.

One possible solution is to combine both methods in a two-hour Bible study. One reading can be chosen to be studied in more depth in the second hour, while the whole section is given the first treatment in the first hour. Remember, whatever you do, keep to the text and help everybody enjoy the challenge.

Introduction

Mark requires no introduction – he is anxious to begin.

I apologize to him for this preamble.

Nothing is known of the author. Tradition has it that the Gospel was written in Rome around AD 70 when the Temple in Jerusalem was destroyed by Titus during the Zealot uprising. That event was traumatic to both Jews and the emerging Christian Church and resulted in this new form of literature called a 'Gospel' or 'good news'. Mark was probably the inventor of this genre, and it is certain that Matthew and probably Luke had copies of Mark when they wrote their versions of the good news.

Tradition stemming from a fourth-century bishop, Eusebius of Caesarea, tells of an elder called Papias. He describes Mark as the secretary of Peter who wrote down what Peter remembered but 'not in order'. Scholars are divided as to how accurate this might be. It rather sounds as if Papias favours Luke who tells us he wrote an 'orderly account', which suggests Mark was less organized. This may explain why, until recent times, Mark was the least read of all the four Gospels. Whatever the facts, the Gospel of Mark is the shortest, the most urgent and the most challenging Gospel we have. Written, as it was, during a time of great change and uncertainty, when all the old respected structures were crumbling, it wrestles with the central issues about the meaning of life, of hope and the possibility of a new beginning. Despite overwhelming odds Mark is convinced that he is conveying good news. The big issue is – can anyone receive it and if so, will they put it into practice?

Let Mark begin . . .

PART I

SECTION I

OPEN TO THE MESSAGE

Mark Tells Us Who Jesus Is

Mark 1.1–13

¹**The beginning of the gospel about Jesus Christ, the Son of God.**
²It is written in Isaiah the prophet: "I will send my messenger ahead of you, who will prepare your way" -
³"a voice of one calling in the desert, 'Prepare the way for the Lord, make straight paths for him.'"
⁴And so John came, baptising in the desert region and preaching a baptism of repentance for the forgiveness of sins. ⁵The whole Judean countryside and all the people of Jerusalem went out to him. Confessing their sins, they were baptised by him in the Jordan River. ⁶John wore clothing made of camel's hair, with a leather belt round his waist, and he ate locusts and wild honey. ⁷And this was his message: "After me will come one more powerful than I, the thongs of whose sandals I am not worthy to stoop down and untie. ⁸I baptise you with water, but he will baptise you with the Holy Spirit."
⁹At that time Jesus came from Nazareth in Galilee and was baptised by John in the Jordan. ¹⁰As Jesus was coming up out of the water, he saw heaven being torn open and the Spirit descending on him like a dove. ¹¹And a voice came from heaven: "You are my Son, whom I love; with you I am well pleased."
¹²At once the Spirit sent him out into the desert, ¹³and he was in the desert for forty days, being tempted by Satan. He was with the wild animals, and angels attended him.

Mark begins with a banner headline. He lets us in on a secret: 'The beginning of the gospel about Jesus Christ, the Son of God'. We know exactly who he believes Jesus to be and that this is good news. This is the theme of his Gospel although many characters in the Gospel will not understand the truth. The rest of the Gospel will expound this belief through narrative, and through the teachings of Jesus. The story will end with a Roman soldier making the same statement (15.39 'Surely this man was a son of God!').

The scene is set with the appearance of John the Baptist whose sole purpose is to point to someone more powerful than himself (v7). Cast in the role of Elijah, he prepares the way both as a road builder (v3) and as a baptizer (vv4–5). Those who came to faith in Jesus as the Christ, the Son of God, will have made this proclamation at baptism. It is fitting that this Gospel begins with the rite of baptism and with the promise of the Spirit which enables people to follow Christ. Once Jesus is baptized, the heavenly voice confirms his identity (v11) and immediately the Spirit-filled Jesus is driven into the desert to wrestle with Satan.

- Who is Jesus? How would we describe him?

- Is he good news for the people among whom we live?

- How can we, as a believing community, make him known?

- Mark has John the Baptist making preparations. Does the Christian message need some basic spadework today? Does the ground need levelling? How can we do it?

- Why does Mark omit to tell us about the birth and boyhood of Jesus? Is it more important to begin with baptism?

- What is our policy on baptism? Are we ready to turn people away or invite them to share the good news?

- Are we a Spirit-filled people in whom God is well pleased?

- Are we ready for the struggle with the forces of evil?

- Can we walk into a spiritual desert, armed with God's Spirit, and face wild beasts?

2

Jesus Tells Us of the Kingdom of God

Mark 1.14–28

[14]**After John was put in prison, Jesus went** into Galilee, proclaiming the good news of God. [15]"The time has come," he said. "The kingdom of God is near. Repent and believe the good news!"

[16]As Jesus walked beside the Sea of Galilee, he saw Simon and his brother Andrew casting a net into the lake, for they were fishermen. [17]"Come, follow me," Jesus said, "and I will make you fishers of men." [18]At once they left their nets and followed him.

[19]When he had gone a little farther, he saw James son of Zebedee and his brother John in a boat, preparing their nets. [20]Without delay he called them, and they left their father Zebedee in the boat with the hired men and followed him.

[21]They went to Capernaum, and when the Sabbath came, Jesus went into the synagogue and began to teach. [22]The people were amazed at his teaching, because he taught them as one who had authority, not as the teachers of the law. [23]Just then a man in their synagogue who was possessed by an evil spirit cried out, [24]"What do you want with us, Jesus of Nazareth? Have you come to destroy us? I know who you are - the Holy One of God!" [25]"Be quiet!" said Jesus sternly. "Come out of him!" [26]The evil spirit shook the man violently and came out of him with a shriek.

[27]The people were all so amazed that they asked each other, "What is this? A new teaching - and with authority! He even gives orders to evil spirits and they obey him." [28]News about him spread quickly over the whole region of Galilee.

Suddenly we come down to earth. Jesus breaks into the narrative announcing his purpose. The proclaimer proclaims the gospel (vv14–15). There is no time to lose. God is present and demands a response and a belief in the good news.

Mark is full of urgency. Things happen immediately. Jesus walks beside the Sea of Galilee and people leave their nets to become disciples. One theme of Mark's Gospel is a readiness to follow Jesus. This opening story perfectly illustrates what is expected in response to the good news.

4

The town of Capernaum becomes the base for Jesus' operations. Here Jesus displays more of that irresistible charismatic authority which astonishes those who encounter it, and which calls forth an immediate response. The bystanders recognize his authoritative teaching. So does the man possessed. If the crowds recognize the authority of Jesus, the supernatural world knows who he really is – the 'Holy One of God' (v24). Jesus must do battle with the forces of evil. This episode in the synagogue contains all the elements of struggle that Jesus will encounter as he makes God's presence real among his people.

- **What is the kingdom of God?**

- **How urgent is it for us to proclaim the kingdom of God?**

- **What does repentance mean? Is it a complete turn around?**

- **We use the words 'I repent of my sins' at baptism. What does this mean?**

- **The disciples leave their nets and families to follow Christ. What do we need to walk away from?**

- **What is this authority Jesus has, and how do we recognize it in the church today?**

The Ministry Extends

Mark 1.29–45

²⁹**As soon as they left the synagogue, they** went with James and John to the home of Simon and Andrew. ³⁰Simon's mother-in-law was in bed with a fever, and they told Jesus about her. ³¹So he went to her, took her hand and helped her up. The fever left her and she began to wait on them.

³²That evening after sunset the people brought to Jesus all the sick and demon-possessed. ³³The whole town gathered at the door, ³⁴and Jesus healed many who had various diseases. He also drove out many demons, but he would not let the demons speak because they knew who he was.

³⁵Very early in the morning, while it was still dark, Jesus got up, left the house and went off to a solitary place, where he prayed. ³⁶Simon and his companions went to look for him, ³⁷and when they found him, they exclaimed: "Everyone is looking for you!" ³⁸Jesus replied, "Let us go somewhere else - to the nearby villages - so that I can preach there also. That is why I have come." ³⁹So he travelled throughout Galilee, preaching in their synagogues and driving out demons.

⁴⁰A man with leprosy came to him and begged him on his knees, "If you are willing, you can make me clean."

⁴¹Filled with compassion, Jesus reached out his hand and touched the man. "I am willing," he said. "Be clean!" ⁴²Immediately the leprosy left him and he was cured.

⁴³Jesus sent him away at once with a strong warning: ⁴⁴"See that you don't tell this to anyone. But go, show yourself to the priest and offer the sacrifices that Moses commanded for your cleansing, as a testimony to them." ⁴⁵Instead he went out and began to talk freely, spreading the news. As a result, Jesus could no longer enter a town openly but stayed outside in lonely places. Yet the people still came to him from everywhere.

Mark continues his breathless pace as Jesus immediately leaves the synagogue to be with his disciples. A house or *'insula'*, which may have been the home of Simon Peter, has been excavated alongside the synagogue at Capernaum. In the home of Simon and Andrew, Jesus restores Simon's mother-in-law, and is besieged by the sick of the town who crowd about the door. Mark reveals a very human Jesus needing rest and refreshment, but constantly disturbed by the pressing needs of humanity. Even his early morning prayer time is interrupted. 'Everyone is looking for you', is their plea (v37). Jesus readily embarks on a preaching tour of the region using the synagogues as a platform for his message. Those who recognize him are forbidden to make it known (vv33, 44) but they are unable to keep silent, and Jesus is pursued by a populace who flock to see him as they would a modern pop star.

- How important is it for us not to have our times of quiet for prayer interrupted?

- Can we achieve a balance between prayer and responding to urgent needs?

- Is this picture of a popular Jesus, sought after by adoring crowds, somewhat idealized by Mark to make the point that Jesus attracts a following?

- What are the dangers of popularity? How do young people deal with such adulation? Does it turn heads and invite criticism?

- Why does Jesus insist on silence? Is he concerned that his identity might be misconstrued? What sort of Messiah is he?

4

Authority to Forgive Sins

Mark 2.1–12

¹**A few days later, when Jesus again entered** Capernaum, the people heard that he had come home. ²So many gathered that there was no room left, not even outside the door, and he preached the word to them. ³Some men came, bringing to him a paralytic, carried by four of them. ⁴Since they could not get him to Jesus because of the crowd, they made an opening in the roof above Jesus and, after digging through it, lowered the mat the paralysed man was lying on. ⁵When Jesus saw their faith, he said to the paralytic, "Son, your sins are forgiven."

⁶Now some teachers of the law were sitting there, thinking to themselves, ⁷"Why does this fellow talk like that? He's blaspheming! Who can forgive sins but God alone?"

⁸Immediately Jesus knew in his spirit that this was what they were thinking in their hearts, and he said to them, "Why are you thinking these things? ⁹Which is easier: to say to the paralytic, 'Your sins are forgiven,' or to say, 'Get up, take your mat and walk'? ¹⁰But that you may know that the Son of Man has authority on earth to forgive sins. . . ." He said to the paralytic, ¹¹"I tell you, get up, take your mat and go home." ¹²He got up, took his mat and walked out in full view of them all. This amazed everyone and they praised God, saying, "We have never seen anything like this!"

Jesus returns 'home' to Capernaum (v1) to preach the gospel (good news). Again the crowds gather so that it is impossible to enter the house. This will not deter determined disciples who need to get to Jesus. Four of them carry a paralytic friend on to the roof, breaking it open, to lower him down at the feet of Jesus. Jesus immediately responds to such faith and this sets in motion a chain of events which will result in his death on a charge of blasphemy. If God is present in Jesus, liberating humanity, then those opposed to such 'a new teaching' will do their best to destroy it. The authority represented by Jesus overcomes the paralysis of sin, and the man takes up his bed and walks (v12). The crowd respond with amazement, glorifying God and testifying to the newness of what they are witnessing (v12). 'We have never seen anything like this!' they exclaim. Mark portrays Jesus as the complete innovator who can break the stereotypical mould.

- How rigid are we in our attitudes? Are we willing to be carried by the faith of others?

- Can we allow ourselves to be placed at the feet of Christ?

- Are we prepared to take risks for our faith? – even to break down barriers?

- Does our pride prevent us from responding to Christ's invitation to take up our bed and walk?

- How suspicious are we of innovation?

- Can we see God at work liberating his frozen people?

- How determined are we to preserve the past in order to paralyse the present and prevent the future from happening?

- Can we recognize God at work in the world? Are we ready to acclaim him?

- Who is this mysterious Son of Man (v10)?

5

Jesus makes
disciples of the outcasts

Mark 2.13–22

¹³**Once again Jesus went out beside the lake.** A large crowd came to him, and he began to teach them. ¹⁴As he walked along, he saw Levi son of Alphaeus sitting at the tax collector's booth. "Follow me," Jesus told him, and Levi got up and followed him.

¹⁵While Jesus was having dinner at Levi's house, many tax collectors and "sinners" were eating with him and his disciples, for there were many who followed him. ¹⁶When the teachers of the law who were Pharisees saw him eating with the "sinners" and tax collectors, they asked his disciples: "Why does he eat with tax collectors and 'sinners'?"

¹⁷On hearing this, Jesus said to them, "It is not the healthy who need a doctor, but the sick. I have not come to call the righteous, but sinners."

¹⁸Now John's disciples and the Pharisees were fasting. Some people came and asked Jesus, "How is it that John's disciples and the disciples of the Pharisees are fasting, but yours are not?"

¹⁹Jesus answered, "How can the guests of the bridegroom fast while he is with them? They cannot, so long as they have him with them. ²⁰But the time will come when the bridegroom will be taken from them, and on that day they will fast.

²¹"No-one sews a patch of unshrunk cloth on an old garment. If he does, the new piece will pull away from the old, making the tear worse. ²²And no-one pours new wine into old wineskins. If he does, the wine will burst the skins, and both the wine and the wineskins will be ruined. No, he pours new wine into new wineskins."

This Gospel began with a road-building programme (1.3). Here we have Jesus on the main east–west route, which ran along the north shore of Galilee. He breaks new ground by calling a complete outsider to follow him. Again the response is immediate. Levi leaves his hated profession and follows Jesus. This is an excuse for a party, and it looks from the text as if Jesus is the host. The guests all recline together so this is some celebration. The spectacle of Jesus mixing with tax collectors and sinners causes great offence, and the pious Pharisees complain, citing John the Baptist as an example of good practice. Jesus reminds them that he has come with the good news that no one is excluded from the forgiving grace of God. The followers of Jesus have something to celebrate. Jesus has overturned the tables on those who shun the outsider – everyone is invited to the Lord's supper. The only division is created by those who reject the invitation. Again the shadow of the cross falls over this passage in the reference to the time for 'the bridegroom [to] be taken away' (v20) and the tearing of cloth and bursting of wineskins (vv21–2). This teacher and his followers will offend old values and they will suffer for it.

- **Are there many attracted to Jesus today but put off by the Church?**

- **Who would we exclude from the Lord's supper and why?**

- **Are we offended by the behaviour of those who have newly found Christ?**

- **How obsessed are we by rules and regulations?**

- **Are we prepared for the pain of tearing and bursting that Jesus' teaching will involve?**

- **Can the old be adapted to accommodate the new? It would appear from this passage that they cannot!**

SECTION 2

OPEN TO THE CALL

6

Sabbath Conflicts

Mark 2.23—3.12

²³**One Sabbath Jesus was going through the cornfields, and as his disciples walked along, they began to pick some ears of corn.** ²⁴The Pharisees said to him, "Look, why are they doing what is unlawful on the Sabbath?" ²⁵He answered, "Have you never read what David did when he and his companions were hungry and in need? ²⁶In the days of Abiathar the high priest, he entered the house of God and ate the consecrated bread, which is lawful only for priests to eat. And he also gave some to his companions." ²⁷Then he said to them, "The Sabbath was made for man, not man for the Sabbath. ²⁸So the Son of Man is Lord even of the Sabbath." ³·¹Another time he went into the synagogue, and a man with a shrivelled hand was there. ²Some of them were looking for a reason to accuse Jesus, so they watched him closely to see if he would heal him on the Sabbath. ³Jesus said to the man with the shrivelled hand, "Stand up in front of everyone." ⁴Then Jesus asked them, "Which is lawful on the Sabbath: to do good or to do evil, to save life or to kill?" But they remained silent. ⁵He looked round at them in anger and, deeply distressed at their stubborn hearts, said to the man, "Stretch out your hand." He stretched it out, and his hand was completely restored. ⁶Then the Pharisees went out and began to plot with the Herodians how they might kill Jesus. ⁷Jesus withdrew with his disciples to the lake, and a large crowd from Galilee followed. ⁸When they heard all he was doing, many people came to him from Judea, Jerusalem, Idumea, and the regions across the Jordan and around Tyre and Sidon. ⁹Because of the crowd he told his disciples to have a small boat ready for him, to keep the people from crowding him. ¹⁰For he had healed many, so that those with diseases were pushing forward to touch him. ¹¹Whenever the evil spirits saw him, they fell down before him and cried out, "You are the Son of God." ¹²But he gave them strict orders not to tell who he was.

The head-on collision continues with the Pharisees who object to the behaviour of Jesus and his disciples on the Sabbath. This time they are breaking the rules openly. Jesus comes under direct attack in the grainfields and responds with a counter question and a reference to Scripture (vv25–8). His second answer is more convincing: 'The

Sabbath was made for man, not man for the Sabbath' (v27), reminding his critics of first principles. Jesus is so confident that he is doing God's will that he can talk of himself as the Son of Man who is Lord even of the Sabbath (v28).

This new authority is demonstrated in the healing of the man with a withered hand – again on the Sabbath. The Pharisees do not openly oppose Jesus in the synagogue, but they are there watching and waiting, collecting evidence to destroy him. Jesus directly confronts their prejudice and hardness of heart with a question about saving life on the Sabbath. He is grieved and angered by their sullen attitude. The man is healed and immediately the wheels are set in motion which will have Jesus eliminated.

The ordinary people who have heard him gladly come from far and wide (3.8). They are in strong contrast with the carping critics of official Judaism. So great is the crush that Jesus makes innovative use of a boat from which to preach.

- Is there a distinction today between those who seek religious truths and those who believe they are protecting them?

- Can we get back to first principles about a God who loves us, heals us and restores us?

- Is there a self-destruct mechanism in the Church that stifles innovation?

- Are we sourly sitting on the sidelines, ever ready to criticize and plot when we are offended by new insights into the truth?

7

The Twelve Are Appointed
and Misunderstanding Follows

Mark 3.13–30

¹³**Jesus went up on a mountainside and** called to him those he wanted, and they came to him. ¹⁴He appointed twelve - designating them apostles - that they might be with him and that he might send them out to preach ¹⁵and to have authority to drive out demons. ¹⁶These are the twelve he appointed: Simon (to whom he gave the name Peter); ¹⁷James son of Zebedee and his brother John (to them he gave the name Boanerges, which means Sons of Thunder); ¹⁸Andrew, Philip, Bartholomew, Matthew, Thomas, James son of Alphaeus, Thaddaeus, Simon the Zealot ¹⁹and Judas Iscariot, who betrayed him. ²⁰Then Jesus entered a house, and again a crowd gathered, so that he and his disciples were not even able to eat. ²¹When his family heard about this, they went to take charge of him, for they said, "He is out of his mind." ²²And the teachers of the law who came down from Jerusalem said, "He is possessed by Beelzebub! By the prince of demons he is driving out demons."

²³So Jesus called them and spoke to them in parables: "How can Satan drive out Satan? ²⁴If a kingdom is divided against itself, that kingdom cannot stand. ²⁵If a house is divided against itself, that house cannot stand. ²⁶And if Satan opposes himself and is divided, he cannot stand; his end has come. ²⁷In fact, no-one can enter a strong man's house and carry off his possessions unless he first ties up the strong man. Then he can rob his house. ²⁸I tell you the truth, all the sins and blasphemies of men will be forgiven them. ²⁹But whoever blasphemes against the Holy Spirit will never be forgiven; he is guilty of an eternal sin." ³⁰He said this because they were saying, "He has an evil spirit."

The Twelve are a symbolic number for a new Israel. Is Jesus standing over against the old Israel? He is certainly leading a new revolutionary community. It is plain from Mark's Gospel that the circle of Jesus' followers is much wider than the Twelve and they may not have had the status we now ascribe to them. The role of a disciple was to be with Jesus and to be sent out to preach (v14) and authoritatively to cast out demons (v15). Mark again reminds us of the cross by referring to one of the disciples as the agent of betrayal. Jesus returns home (presumably to his base in Capernaum) where difficulties continue. His friends try to restrain him (v21), a deputation from Jerusalem accuse him of devilry. Jesus confronts them and talks of binding the 'strong man'. He has already overcome Satan (1.13) and plundered his goods by liberating men and women from his power. The Pharisees are in danger of blaspheming against God's Spirit in the ministry of Jesus (v29). By being so bloody-minded they have condemned themselves. The irony is they will bring a blasphemy charge against Jesus.

• **Do we see our discipleship in terms of being with Jesus?**

• **What does 'have authority to drive out demons' (v15) mean? Is it an ability to name and confront evil?**

• **The friends and family of Jesus tried to restrain him (v21). What does this tell us about Jesus' single-mindedness?**

• **Do we have the grace and conviction to stand up for what we believe is the truth, even in the face of overwhelming criticism?**

• **Is there a well-meaning plot in religious circles to suppress the kind of Jesus we are encountering in this Gospel?**

8

Family Opposition

Mark 3.31–5

³¹**Then Jesus' mother and brothers arrived.** Standing outside, they sent someone in to call him. ³²A crowd was sitting around him, and they told him, "Your mother and brothers are outside looking for you."
³³"Who are my mother and my brothers?" he asked. ³⁴Then he looked at those seated in a circle around him and said, "Here are my mother and my brothers! ³⁵Whoever does God's will is my brother and sister and mother."

The friends and relatives who appeared in v21 now arrive in order to restrain Jesus who, as far as they are concerned, is out of his mind. It is almost as if they want him arrested, so strong is the Greek word used in v21. Perhaps they account his madness as due to demon possession. If so they would be in agreement with the scribes.

It shocks us to discover that Mary is in such company! We have been brought up on a diet of Luke's Gospel where Mary is afforded more respect. As far as Mark is concerned, she and the family of Jesus have completely misunderstood him and are definitely outside the circle of disciples (v31). Those who sit at Jesus' feet are those willing to learn – the family exclude themselves by remaining outside. Jesus therefore looks to his disciples as his new family (v35).

This is a very difficult passage. The point being made is that Jesus is rejected and misunderstood both by the nation and his own people. He, therefore, looks to those who will do the will of God to be the new kingdom community. There is a parallel saying to this in the *Gospel of Thomas* (99): 'Those here who do the will of my Father are my brothers and my mother. These are they who will enter the kingdom of my Father.'

- What does discipleship mean for us?

- How do we deal with family opposition?

- Is there a danger of taking this message too far and cutting ourselves off from family ties?

- Do we need to see this passage as an example of Jesus' isolation and rejection rather than read into it our own family problems?

The Parable of the Sower

Mark 4.1–20

¹**Again Jesus began to teach by the lake.** The crowd that gathered round him was so large that he got into a boat and sat in it out on the lake, while all the people were along the shore at the water's edge. ²He taught them many things by parables, and in his teaching said: ³"Listen! A farmer went out to sow his seed. ⁴As he was scattering the seed, some fell along the path, and the birds came and ate it up. ⁵Some fell on rocky places, where it did not have much soil. It sprang up quickly, because the soil was shallow. ⁶But when the sun came up, the plants were scorched, and they withered because they had no root. ⁷Other seed fell among thorns, which grew up and choked the plants, so that they did not bear grain. ⁸Still other seed fell on good soil. It came up, grew and produced a crop, multiplying thirty, sixty, or even a hundred times."

⁹Then Jesus said, "He who has ears to hear, let him hear."

¹⁰When he was alone, the Twelve and the others around him asked him about the parables. ¹¹He told them, "The secret of the kingdom of God has been given to you. But to those on the outside everything is said in parables ¹²so that, "'they may be ever seeing but never perceiving, and ever hearing but never understanding; otherwise they might turn and be forgiven!'"

¹³Then Jesus said to them, "Don't you understand this parable? How then will you understand any parable? ¹⁴The farmer sows the word. ¹⁵Some people are like seed along the path, where the word is sown. As soon as they hear it, Satan comes and takes away the word that was sown in them. ¹⁶Others, like seed sown on rocky places, hear the word and at once receive it with joy. ¹⁷But since they have no root, they last only a short time. When trouble or persecution comes because of the word, they quickly fall away. ¹⁸Still others, like seed sown among thorns, hear the word; ¹⁹but the worries of this life, the deceitfulness of wealth and the desires for other things come in and choke the word, making it unfruitful. ²⁰Others, like seed sown on good soil, hear the word, accept it, and produce a crop - thirty, sixty or even a hundred times what was sown."

Mark has Jesus in his favourite location – teaching beside the lake. The crowds gather about him eager to hear this 'new teaching' (1.27) from a boat moored near the shore so that Jesus, as Mark has it, sat in the sea. The point he is making in his rather clumsy Greek is that Jesus is adopting the posture of a teacher and for the first time we are given a sample of his teaching. Mark has no equivalent to Matthew's Sermon on the Mount, and it is true to say his short Gospel contains less teaching material than the others. Nevertheless, Mark emphasizes in his narrative that Jesus is a teacher with a new teaching. The teaching we have in Mark comes largely in the form of parable, a story drawn from everyday life that is meant to tease its hearers about the kingdom of God. Parables both reveal and conceal the kingdom, depending on the openness of those who have 'ears to hear' (v9). This first parable is an introduction. There are those who will understand and respond and there are those who will not (v12), just as there are those who will receive Jesus and those who will reject him. The parables are about matters of life and death. Those who recognize this will choose life and accept both the kingdom itself and the one who proclaims it.

- **How can we proclaim the kingdom of God in a language people recognize?**

- **Do we acknowledge the importance of storytelling in communicating the gospel?**

- **How deaf are we to this new teaching which demands a response?**

- **Are we too choked with cares and too lacking in depth to bring forth fruit? If Jesus can rebuke his disciples for their failure to respond (v13) he can rebuke us!**

More Secrets
of the Kingdom Revealed

Mark 4.21–34

²¹**He said to them, "Do you bring in a lamp** to put it under a bowl or a bed? Instead, don't you put it on its stand? ²²For whatever is hidden is meant to be disclosed, and whatever is concealed is meant to be brought out into the open. ²³If anyone has ears to hear, let him hear."

²⁴"Consider carefully what you hear," he continued. "With the measure you use, it will be measured to you - and even more. ²⁵Whoever has will be given more; whoever does not have, even what he has will be taken from him."

²⁶He also said, "This is what the kingdom of God is like. A man scatters seed on the ground. ²⁷Night and day, whether he sleeps or gets up, the seed sprouts and grows, though he does not know how. ²⁸All by itself the soil produces corn - first the stalk, then the ear, then the full grain in the ear. ²⁹As soon as the grain is ripe, he puts the sickle to it, because the harvest has come."

³⁰Again he said, "What shall we say the kingdom of God is like, or what parable shall we use to describe it? ³¹It is like a mustard seed, which is the smallest seed you plant in the ground. ³²Yet when planted, it grows and becomes the largest of all garden plants, with such big branches that the birds of the air can perch in its shade."

³³With many similar parables Jesus spoke the word to them, as much as they could understand. ³⁴He did not say anything to them without using a parable. But when he was alone with his own disciples, he explained everything.

'If you've got it, flaunt it' is the contemporary version about not hiding your light. What does Jesus mean by this and the other strange sayings in the passage? Maybe the best commentary comes from the opening verses of St John's Gospel: 'the light shines in the darkness, but the darkness has not overcome it' (John 1.5). If Jesus is the light, he must not be hidden by those opposed to him. We must see and hear (vv23–4) him for what he is and respond accordingly. Those who do not, who wish to sweep him and his teachings under the carpet – or under the bed (v21) – will be bereft of the kingdom which will be given to those who have received Jesus' message (v25). The word is meant to be heard, the light to give light and the seed to grow. Nothing can prevent this. God's purposes will come to fruition. This is the message of the kingdom which Jesus proclaims and it is uniquely linked to the one who proclaims it.

The parables are a challenge, but those who respond will understand more readily the secrets of the kingdom (v34).

- **The two parables of the kingdom in this passage suggest that whatever the kingdom is, it grows quietly and secretly until one day, we discover it has spread to enormous proportions. Can we discern the mysterious, almost secret growth of the kingdom of God in our lives?**

- **Is there a mystery in the link between the kingdom and the inevitability of growth in the natural world?**

- **Can we not just allow the kingdom to grow and flourish?**

- **How ready are we to place a candle on a candlestick? Is the church too beset with secrecy?**

SECTION 3

OPEN TO REJECTION

11

A Storm on the Lake - Power over Wind and Wave

Mark 4.35–41

[35]**That day when evening came, he said to** his disciples, "Let us go over to the other side." [36]Leaving the crowd behind, they took him along, just as he was, in the boat. There were also other boats with him. [37]A furious squall came up, and the waves broke over the boat, so that it was nearly swamped. [38]Jesus was in the stern, sleeping on a cushion. The disciples woke him and said to him, "Teacher, don't you care if we drown?" [39]He got up, rebuked the wind and said to the waves, "Quiet! Be still!" Then the wind died down and it was completely calm. [40]He said to his disciples, "Why are you so afraid? Do you still have no faith?" [41]They were terrified and asked each other, "Who is this? Even the wind and the waves obey him!"

The crowds are left behind and the disciples invited to 'the other side' of the lake (v35). We now enter a section of four miracles, but their purpose is the same as the parables – to reveal the authority of Jesus. It is significant that the first miracle should take place on the Sea of Galilee. The waters of chaos are calmed by Jesus just as God was able to breathe calm into chaos waters at creation (Gen. 1) or take control in Psalm 107.23–32 or Jonah 1.1–16. All the more remarkable that fishermen should be so terrified while Jesus sleeps on a pillow in the stern. The whole incident turns on the central question of this Gospel. 'Who is this?' (v41). Who is Jesus? What does he represent, 'even the wind and sea obey him'?

The fear of the disciples arises out of their lack of faith: they have mislaid it – like the car keys. They need to find it again. They have glimpsed a trust and faith in Jesus but they easily panic. There is no need to fear – the faith that is growing in them will overcome fear.

NB This Gospel ends on a note of fear when the women discover Jesus is risen. That fear was overcome by faith to proclaim the gospel.

- Are we liable to panic when the going gets tough?

- Is our faith often mislaid, stunted and unsure?

- Can we calm ourselves down when we hear the voice of Jesus say 'Quiet! Be still' (v39)?

- Is God really in control or does he require our co-operation for changes to take effect?

- Do we inhibit God's work when we are too fearful to co-operate with him?

12

Power over Unclean Spirits

Mark 5.1–20

¹**They went across the lake to the region of the Gerasenes.** ²When Jesus got out of the boat, a man with an evil spirit came from the tombs to meet him. ³This man lived in the tombs, and no-one could bind him any more, not even with a chain. ⁴For he had often been chained hand and foot, but he tore the chains apart and broke the irons on his feet. No-one was strong enough to subdue him. ⁵Night and day among the tombs and in the hills he would cry out and cut himself with stones. ⁶When he saw Jesus from a distance, he ran and fell on his knees in front of him. ⁷He shouted at the top of his voice, "What do you want with me, Jesus, Son of the Most High God? Swear to God that you won't torture me!" ⁸For Jesus had said to him, "Come out of this man, you evil spirit!"

⁹Then Jesus asked him, "What is your name?" "My name is Legion," he replied, "for we are many." ¹⁰And he begged Jesus again and again not to send them out of the area.

¹¹A large herd of pigs was feeding on the nearby hillside. ¹²The demons begged Jesus, "Send us among the pigs; allow us to go into them." ¹³He gave them permission, and the evil spirits came out and went into the pigs. The herd, about two thousand in number, rushed down the steep bank into the lake and were drowned.

¹⁴Those tending the pigs ran off and reported this in the town and countryside, and the people went out to see what had happened. ¹⁵When they came to Jesus, they saw the man who had been possessed by the legion of demons, sitting there, dressed and in his right mind; and they were afraid. ¹⁶Those who had seen it told the people what had happened to the demon-possessed man - and told about the pigs as well. ¹⁷Then the people began to plead with Jesus to leave their region.

¹⁸As Jesus was getting into the boat, the man who had been demon-possessed begged to go with him. ¹⁹Jesus did not let him, but said, "Go home to your family and tell them how much the Lord has done for you, and how he has had mercy on you." ²⁰So the man went away and began to tell in the Decapolis how much Jesus had done for him. And all the people were amazed.

Having crossed over to the other side of what Mark calls the 'lake', Jesus enters pagan country. We may ask ourselves the question, 'What is a good kosher boy like Jesus doing in such a place – a graveyard, peopled with pigs, pagans and a naked, wild man who is possessed?' All of this is completely off-limits for a law-abiding Jew. In this second miracle, the authority of Jesus and the kingdom he represents is extended both over the ragings of nature and the unnatural deranged demoniac. The common factor is that both the forces of nature and the unnatural demoniac recognize the authority Jesus represents. This is in sharp contrast to the vacillations of fearful disciples.

There is something of the oriental enjoyment of tale-telling in this incident with its detailed description of the 'legion' that possesses this poor man. The point of the story is the power Jesus has to enable men and women to be clothed in their right mind (v15). We are reminded of the prodigal son, also in the company of swine, coming to his senses.

The fear that is engendered by this incident prevents the pagan population coming to faith in Jesus and they ask him to leave (v17). The restored man is commissioned to spread the good news among his own people by way of preparing for the Gentile mission which will follow after the resurrection. That a naked man might be restored to new life reminds us of what will become the experience of Jesus on Golgotha.

- **Are we prepared to make sorties into unknown territory to befriend and help the outcast?**

- **How prepared are we to overcome prejudice and fear in getting alongside the homeless and deranged?**

- **Can such people be 'ransomed, healed, restored, forgiven' and so sing God's praises?**

- **Are we responsible for keeping them fettered and isolated from normal society by our stand-offish attitude?**

- **How does society care for such people?**

13

Power over Death

Mark 5.21–43

²¹**When Jesus had again crossed over by** boat to the other side of the lake, a large crowd gathered round him while he was by the lake. ²²Then one of the synagogue rulers, named Jairus, came there. Seeing Jesus, he fell at his feet ²³and pleaded earnestly with him, "My little daughter is dying. Please come and put your hands on her so that she will be healed and live." ²⁴So Jesus went with him. A large crowd followed and pressed around him. ²⁵And a woman was there who had been subject to bleeding for twelve years. ²⁶She had suffered a great deal under the care of many doctors and had spent all she had, yet instead of getting better she grew worse. ²⁷When she heard about Jesus, she came up behind him in the crowd and touched his cloak, ²⁸because she thought, "If I just touch his clothes, I will be healed." ²⁹Immediately her bleeding stopped and she felt in her body that she was freed from her suffering.

³⁰At once Jesus realised that power had gone out from him. He turned around in the crowd and asked, "Who touched my clothes?"

³¹"You see the people crowding against you," his disciples answered, "and yet you can ask, 'Who touched me?'"

³²But Jesus kept looking around to see who had done it. ³³Then the woman, knowing what had happened to her, came and fell at his feet

and, trembling with fear, told him the whole truth. ³⁴He said to her, "Daughter, your faith has healed you. Go in peace and be freed from your suffering."

³⁵While Jesus was still speaking, some men came from the house of Jairus, the synagogue ruler. "Your daughter is dead," they said. "Why bother the teacher any more?"

³⁶Ignoring what they said, Jesus told the synagogue ruler, "Don't be afraid; just believe."

³⁷He did not let anyone follow him except Peter, James and John the brother of James. ³⁸When they came to the home of the synagogue ruler, Jesus saw a commotion, with people crying and wailing loudly. ³⁹He went in and said to them, "Why all this commotion and wailing? The child is not dead but asleep." ⁴⁰But they laughed at him.

After he put them all out, he took the child's father and mother and the disciples who were with him, and went in where the child was. ⁴¹He took her by the hand and said to her, *"Talitha koum!"* (which means, "Little girl, I say to you, get up!"). ⁴²Immediately the girl stood up and walked around (she was twelve years old). At this they were completely astonished. ⁴³He gave strict orders not to let anyone know about this, and told them to give her something to eat.

Mark loves a sandwich. He tells a number of stories in which a sub-plot is embedded like the filling in a roll (compare 3.21–35 and 11.12–25).

Here we are meant to see that Jesus has power not only to restore people to a right mind but also to give them life. The child is either dead or in a coma, and the woman as good as dead in that she has no life in normal society. Outsiders – those who are as good as dead – are brought the reassurance of new life.

Jesus is back in familiar territory. We are not told where. Possibly the scene is the Capernaum synagogue where we have been before (3.1). Jairus, unlike the delegation from Jerusalem, recognizes Jesus as a healer and a provider of life (v23). Jesus readily responds, but on the way encounters a woman who, because of her condition, puts her and those who come into contact with her in some danger. She takes a risk in approaching Jesus. He invites her to share her story so as to demonstrate that no one is beyond God's help. The woman's faith has overcome the taboo of fear and she can go in peace (v34).

Meanwhile the weeping and wailing signals the death of the child. Jesus reassures Jairus not to fear 'just believe' (v36). He is to keep faith with Jesus the lifegiver. For both of them the child is merely sleeping (as Lazarus was in John 11). The miracle of this story cannot fully be understood until after the resurrection which it prefigures. Hence Jesus orders them not to tell anyone (v43). Jesus has once again overcome the defiling forces of death and social ostracism.

- **Who are the people we would keep at arm's length in our society?**

- **Can we not see how deadly it is to fall victim to prejudice and fear?**

- **Notice it is women that Jesus restores in these stories. So often throughout history they have been ignored. Is this still happening in our society today?**

- **How much are we affected by social convention and political correctness?**

14

Rejection
Followed by a Commission

Mark 6.1–13

¹Jesus left there and went to his home town, accompanied by his disciples. ²When the Sabbath came, he began to teach in the synagogue, and many who heard him were amazed.

"Where did this man get these things?" they asked. "What's this wisdom that has been given him, that he even does miracles! ³Isn't this the carpenter? Isn't this Mary's son and the brother of James, Joseph, Judas and Simon? Aren't his sisters here with us?" And they took offence at him.

⁴Jesus said to them, "Only in his home town, among his relatives and in his own house is a prophet without honour." ⁵He could not do any miracles there, except lay his hands on a few sick people and heal them. ⁶And he was amazed at their lack of faith.

Then Jesus went round teaching from village to village. ⁷Calling the Twelve to him, he sent them out two by two and gave them authority over evil spirits. ⁸These were his instructions: "Take nothing for the journey except a staff - no bread, no bag, no money in your belts. ⁹Wear sandals but not an extra tunic. ¹⁰Whenever you enter a house, stay there until you leave that town. ¹¹And if any place will not welcome you or listen to you, shake the dust off your feet when you leave, as a testimony against them."

¹²They went out and preached that people should repent. ¹³They drove out many demons and anointed many sick people with oil and healed them.

Jesus visits his home town of Nazareth and, according to his usual pattern, visits the synagogue where he encounters a mixed reception. The local boy, made good, is given short shrift and Jesus deliberately winds up his townsfolk by quoting a well known proverb about a prophet being unacceptable in his own country. They are scandalized by him as were his family in 3.21. This is in direct contrast to the response of Jairus and the woman in the previous story (5.21–43).

There is also a suggestion in this episode that Jesus was considered illegitimate. To describe anyone as the son of his mother alone was to cast doubts on his parentage. The list of brothers and mention of sisters suggests that Mark knew nothing of the supposed perpetual virginity of Mary. Jesus marvels at their lack of faith. Again the best comment comes from John's prologue: 'He came to that which was his own, but his own did not receive him' (John 1.11).

The Twelve are commissioned with authority to announce the kingdom calling for repentance. They are to go unencumbered: no bread or money, just to take a staff, one coat and sandals (which the radical Luke forbids in his version, Luke 9.3). Mark is reflecting the conditions of the preaching missions of his day when the gospel was spread like wildfire by such itinerant preachers. We are reminded of the preaching friars of the thirteenth and fourteenth centuries who made a similar impact by taking this passage more seriously than we do today.

- **Does the Church need to travel light if the Gospel is to have more impact?**
- **Is there a need for Christian men and women to become itinerants for the sake of the kingdom?**
- **How do we cope with rejection and a refusal to listen?**
- **Can we learn to move on and recapture the sense of urgency in this passage?**

15

John the Baptist Is Executed

Mark 6.14–29

14King Herod heard about this, for Jesus' name had become well known. Some were saying, "John the Baptist has been raised from the dead, and that is why miraculous powers are at work in him."

15Others said, "He is Elijah."

And still others claimed, "He is a prophet, like one of the prophets of long ago."

16But when Herod heard this, he said, "John, the man I beheaded, has been raised from the dead!"

17For Herod himself had given orders to have John arrested, and he had him bound and put in prison. He did this because of Herodias, his brother Philip's wife, whom he had married. 18For John had been saying to Herod, "It is not lawful for you to have your brother's wife." 19So Herodias nursed a grudge against John and wanted to kill him. But she was not able to, 20because Herod feared John and protected him, knowing him to be a righteous and holy man. When Herod heard John, he was greatly puzzled; yet he liked to listen to him.

21Finally the opportune time came. On his birthday Herod gave a banquet for his high officials and military commanders and the leading men of Galilee. 22When the daughter of Herodias came in and danced, she pleased Herod and his dinner guests.

The king said to the girl, "Ask me for anything you want, and I'll give it to you." 23And he promised her with an oath, "Whatever you ask I will give you, up to half my kingdom."

24She went out and said to her mother, "What shall I ask for?"

"The head of John the Baptist," she answered. 25At once the girl hurried in to the king with the request: "I want you to give me right now the head of John the Baptist on a platter."

26The king was greatly distressed, but because of his oaths and his dinner guests, he did not want to refuse her. 27So he immediately sent an executioner with orders to bring John's head. The man went, beheaded John in the prison, 28and brought back his head on a platter. He presented it to the girl, and she gave it to her mother. 29On hearing of this, John's disciples came and took his body and laid it in a tomb.

Here we have another of Mark's sandwiches. Between the sending out of the Twelve and their return, we have this strange oriental tale about the beheading of John the Baptist. This is the only section in the Gospel not dedicated to the person of Jesus. Why is it included? Perhaps because the story of John the Baptist prefigures that of Jesus. Both had a circle of disciples, both engaged in a radical preaching ministry which fell foul of the religious and civil authorities, both were executed on trumped-up charges, even though those who pronounce the death sentence have serious doubts.

Herod Antipas, son of Herod the Great, is presented as a vacillating, decadent despot, beguiled by the charms of a girl dancer like a figure from Scheherazhade's *Thousand and One Nights*. His ambivalent attitude towards John reminds us of Pilate later in this story. Secular authorities appear to be in control, but are they really? They are disturbed by these holy men and their strange new teaching.

The sad little party of disciples who recover and bury John the Baptist reminds us of the scene after the crucifixion.

- **Can we see parallels between this story and the many prisoners of conscience who are incarcerated because of their views?**

- **The scheming intrigue of Herod's court is repeated in many power circles today. How do we liberate those in authority from sycophantic corruption?**

- **Rash promises made to impress lead to disastrous results. How might Herod have extricated himself from this mess?**

SECTION 4

OPEN TO SIGNS

16

The Apostles Return and Five Thousand Are Fed

Mark 6.30–44

³⁰**The apostles gathered round Jesus and** reported to him all they had done and taught. ³¹Then, because so many people were coming and going that they did not even have a chance to eat, he said to them, "Come with me by yourselves to a quiet place and get some rest." ³²So they went away by themselves in a boat to a solitary place. ³³But many who saw them leaving recognised them and ran on foot from all the towns and got there ahead of them. ³⁴When Jesus landed and saw a large crowd, he had compassion on them, because they were like sheep without a shepherd. So he began teaching them many things. ³⁵By this time it was late in the day, so his disciples came to him. "This is a remote place," they said, "and it's already very late. ³⁶Send the people away so that they can go to the surrounding countryside and villages and buy themselves something to eat." ³⁷But he answered, "You give them something to eat."

They said to him, "That would take eight months of a man's wages! Are we to go and spend that much on bread and give it to them to eat?"

³⁸"How many loaves do you have?" he asked. "Go and see."

When they found out, they said, "Five - and two fish."

³⁹Then Jesus directed them to have all the people sit down in groups on the green grass. ⁴⁰So they sat down in groups of hundreds and fifties. ⁴¹Taking the five loaves and the two fish and looking up to heaven, he gave thanks and broke the loaves. Then he gave them to his disciples to set before the people. He also divided the two fish among them all. ⁴²They all ate and were satisfied, ⁴³and the disciples picked up twelve basketfuls of broken pieces of bread and fish. ⁴⁴The number of the men who had eaten was five thousand.

We hear nothing of the success or failure of this mission but Mark does describe the returnees as 'apostles' (v30). This is the only occasion he uses this word, which is the preferred title of Luke for the Twelve. Whereas the term now has overtones of status, it originally denoted 'one who was sent' – an agent acting with the authority of the one who commissioned him with his task.

Jesus wants to reward the Twelve with a sabbatical but, as usual in Mark, the crowds turn up so that there is not even a moment to get a bite to eat (v31). Their vain attempts to find another quiet location are interrupted by even greater hordes. Again Jesus responds with compassion 'because they were like sheep without a shepherd' (v34). As before, Jesus is cast in the role of a teacher.

What follows is the most repeated miracle in the Gospels. The story of the great feeding is told six times – (twice in Mark), and is the only miracle story described by John as well as the Synoptics (Matthew, Mark and Luke). Obviously it is of great significance, being a foretaste of the great messianic banquet which will be enjoyed in the age to come and echoing the story of manna in the wilderness (Exod. 16; Num. 11). Jesus, like a new Moses, feeds his people with teaching and food as well as offering leadership. There are links also with the narrative of the last supper.

The suggestion that the men sit down in organized groups of fifty or one hundred (v40) might mean that this crowd may have been some kind of Zealot army ready to march behind Jesus as their king (as in John 6.15).

- **How are God's people to be fed today?**

- **Do we need to find a desert place, free from distraction, where we might feed on God's Word?**

- **Are the disciples trusting enough? Why do they need to make such gloomy calculations?**

- **Is this miracle of sharing a foretaste of what society could be like if it had a will to distribute the world's resources?**

17

Jesus Walks on Water

Mark 6.45–56

⁴⁵**Immediately Jesus made his disciples get** into the boat and go on ahead of him to Bethsaida, while he dismissed the crowd. ⁴⁶After leaving them, he went up on a mountainside to pray.

⁴⁷When evening came, the boat was in the middle of the lake, and he was alone on land. ⁴⁸He saw the disciples straining at the oars, because the wind was against them. About the fourth watch of the night he went out to them, walking on the lake. He was about to pass by them, ⁴⁹but when they saw him walking on the lake, they thought he was a ghost. They cried out, ⁵⁰because they all saw him and were terrified.

Immediately he spoke to them and said, "Take courage! It is I. Don't be afraid."

⁵¹Then he climbed into the boat with them, and the wind died down. They were completely amazed, ⁵²for they had not understood about the loaves; their hearts were hardened.

⁵³When they had crossed over, they landed at Gennesaret and anchored there. ⁵⁴As soon as they got out of the boat, people recognised Jesus. ⁵⁵They ran throughout that whole region and carried the sick on mats to wherever they heard he was. ⁵⁶And wherever he went - into villages, towns or countryside - they placed the sick in the market-places. They begged him to let them touch even the edge of his cloak, and all who touched him were healed.

Mark has Jesus immediately bundling his disciples into a boat and sending them back across the lake. No reason is given, but we are reminded of the need to escape from the crowd determined to make Jesus a king (John 6.15). As with the John text, Jesus here withdraws into the hills to be alone. In Mark, Jesus then visits the distressed disciples rowing against the wind, in the dark, only to frighten them further. They think he is a ghost. As so often in the Gospels, the disciples are told to have no fear (v50). Jesus joins them in the boat. The wind drops as before.

The story is meant to be understood in terms of an epiphany. Rather like the transfiguration story, later in chapter 9, the disciples are given a glimpse of who Jesus really is. If Jesus has revealed himself as a successor to Moses in feeding his people, then like Moses, he should be able to lead his people across the sea. The Red Sea crossing and the gift of manna are both central to the Exodus story. Had the disciples understood this, they would not be so astonished (v52). They return to the shore only to find the crowds rushing to bring the sick for healing.

- **Can we admit our difficulties with this strange story? Do we lack insight into who Jesus is, rather like the disciples do in this story?**

- **Why is it important for Mark (and the other Evangelists) to demonstrate that Jesus is even greater than Moses?**

- **The ministry of healing is central to Jesus' mission. How can the Church recover this emphasis? Does it point to the resurrection life?**

18

Growing Opposition

Mark 7.1-23

¹**The Pharisees and some of the teachers** of the law who had come from Jerusalem gathered round Jesus and ²saw some of his disciples eating food with hands that were "unclean", that is, unwashed. ³(The Pharisees and all the Jews do not eat unless they give their hands a ceremonial washing, holding to the tradition of the elders. ⁴When they come from the market-place they do not eat unless they wash. And they observe many other traditions, such as the washing of cups, pitchers and kettles.)

⁵So the Pharisees and teachers of the law asked Jesus, "Why don't your disciples live according to the tradition of the elders instead of eating their food with 'unclean' hands?"

⁶He replied, "Isaiah was right when he prophesied about you hypocrites; as it is written:

"'These people honour me with their lips, but their hearts are far from me.

⁷They worship me in vain; their teachings are but rules taught by men.'

⁸You have let go of the commands of God and are holding on to the traditions of men."

⁹And he said to them: "You have a fine way of setting aside the commands of God in order to observe your own traditions! ¹⁰For Moses said, 'Honour your father and your mother,' and, 'Anyone who curses his father or mother

must be put to death.' ¹¹But you say that if a man says to his father or mother: 'Whatever help you might otherwise have received from me is Corban' (that is, a gift devoted to God), ¹²then you no longer let him do anything for his father or mother. ¹³Thus you nullify the word of God by your tradition that you have handed down. And you do many things like that."

¹⁴Again Jesus called the crowd to him and said, "Listen to me, everyone, and understand this. ¹⁵Nothing outside a man can make him 'unclean' by going into him. Rather, it is what comes out of a man that makes him 'unclean'. ¹⁶[If anyone has ears to hear, let him hear.]"

¹⁷After he had left the crowd and entered the house, his disciples asked him about this parable. ¹⁸"Are you so dull?" he asked. "Don't you see that nothing that enters a man from the outside can make him 'unclean'? ¹⁹For it doesn't go into his heart but into his stomach, and then out of his body." (In saying this, Jesus declared all foods "clean".)

²⁰He went on: "What comes out of a man is what makes him 'unclean'. ²¹For from within, out of men's hearts, come evil thoughts, sexual immorality, theft, murder, adultery, ²²greed, malice, deceit, lewdness, envy, slander, arrogance and folly. ²³All these evils come from inside and make a man 'unclean'."

We are back with the theme of official disapproval. Jesus again appears to be flouting the tradition. A regular Jerusalem deputation take him and his disciples to task for disregarding the Pharisaic tradition concerning food laws and not ritually purifying themselves. Jesus reminds them that in elaborating the ritual they are in danger of neglecting to honour God, which is the only thing the law is concerned about. The New Testament is ambivalent about the law, and Mark understands Jesus to abrogate the teaching of the Torah in respect of clean and unclean foods (v20). Possibly the story reflects what was happening in Mark's own community as Christians became more independent of the restraints of Judaism.

Jesus upbraids his disciples for being so dull and lacking in understanding (v18). This may seem to us a little harsh especially as Jesus has been discussing food laws and suddenly switches to the ethics listed in vv21–3. We shall notice a growing pattern of Jesus getting justifiably angry with his disciples who appear obdurate and lacking in common sense.

Mark ends this passage with Jesus emphasizing the radical demands of God for righteousness. This is the first principle of the law and the reason for its being.

- What is our attitude to God's law? Can we argue for exceptions? Do we need to ask what is behind a precept rather than applying it without question?

- Is Jesus too harsh with his critics? Are the Pharisees deserving of this attack?

- Are there ways in which we bend the law for our advantage? Can we see the dangers of this practice?

- Is today's Church rather too bound by tradition as these Pharisees appear to be?

19

A Gentile Girl Is Healed

Mark 7.24–30

²⁴**Jesus left that place and went to the** vicinity of Tyre. He entered a house and did not want anyone to know it; yet he could not keep his presence secret. ²⁵In fact, as soon as she heard about him, a woman whose little daughter was possessed by an evil spirit came and fell at his feet. ²⁶The woman was a Greek, born in Syrian Phoenicia. She begged Jesus to drive the demon out of her daughter.

²⁷"First let the children eat all they want," he told her, "for it is not right to take the children's bread and toss it to their dogs." ²⁸"Yes, Lord," she replied, "but even the dogs under the table eat the children's crumbs." ²⁹Then he told her, "For such a reply, you may go; the demon has left your daughter." ³⁰She went home and found her child lying on the bed, and the demon gone.

Suddenly the scene changes and Jesus is in the far north of Galilee, in Gentile territory. Jesus has just challenged the distinction between clean and unclean foods. He now has to put that distinction into practice with regard to his dealings with Gentiles. Mark knows nothing of the Gentile mission. Indeed he sees Jesus as one who has come to call the lost sheep of the house of Israel. His dealings with the Syro-Phoenician woman are churlish if not rude, (v27), referring to Gentiles as 'dogs' as Jews commonly did. The woman is not fazed by this put-down, but merely persists with her request, politely addressing Jesus as 'Lord' (v28). Like the centurion at the foot of the cross, she displays true insight and faith in Jesus as a provider. For this reply her request is granted and she returns home to find her daughter cured.

By the time Luke writes the Acts of the Apostles, Peter has to learn not to call Gentiles unclean (Acts 10.15). Jesus appears to reassess his Jewish prejudice against Gentiles in this story. Gentiles must have remembered this woman's faith with gratitude.

- If Jesus can reassess a situation and change his attitude, why cannot we do the same about the things which seem inflexible in our life?

- Are we guilty of xenophobia and only too ready to caricature, say, the French or the Germans?

- Does it help if a chief of police states that most muggings are the result of black or white youths attacking harmless citizens? Will it prejudice us against the young people in our society?

- How can we learn to be more inclusive and welcoming to those of different traditions and cultures?

20

Signs and Wonders

Mark 7.31—8.21

³¹**Then Jesus left the vicinity of Tyre and** went through Sidon, down to the Sea of Galilee and into the region of the Decapolis. ³²There some people brought to him a man who was deaf and could hardly talk, and they begged him to place his hand on the man. ³³After he took him aside, away from the crowd, Jesus put his fingers into the man's ears. Then he spat and touched the man's tongue. ³⁴He looked up to heaven and with a deep sigh said to him, *"Ephphatha!"* (which means, "Be opened!"). ³⁵At this, the man's ears were opened, his tongue was loosened and he began to speak plainly.

³⁶Jesus commanded them not to tell anyone. But the more he did so, the more they kept talking about it. ³⁷People were overwhelmed with amazement. "He has done everything well," they said. "He even makes the deaf hear and the mute speak."

⁸·¹During those days another large crowd gathered. Since they had nothing to eat, Jesus called his disciples to him and said, ²"I have compassion for these people; they have already been with me three days and have nothing to eat. ³If I send them home hungry, they will collapse on the way, because some of them have come a long distance."

⁴His disciples answered, "But where in this remote place can anyone get enough bread to feed them?"

⁵"How many loaves do you have?" Jesus asked.

"Seven," they replied.

⁶He told the crowd to sit down on the ground. When he had taken the seven loaves and given thanks, he broke them and gave them to his disciples to set before the people, and they did so. ⁷They had a few small fish as well; he gave thanks for them also and told the disciples to distribute them. ⁸The people ate and were satisfied. Afterwards the disciples picked up seven basketfuls of broken pieces that were left over. ⁹About four thousand men were present. And having sent them away, ¹⁰he got into the boat with his disciples and went to the region of Dalmanutha.

¹¹The Pharisees came and began to question Jesus. To test him, they asked him for a sign from heaven. ¹²He sighed deeply and said, "Why does this generation ask for a miraculous sign? I tell you the truth, no sign will be given to it." ¹³Then he left them, got back into the boat and crossed to the other side.

¹⁴The disciples had forgotten to bring bread, except for one loaf they had with them in the boat. ¹⁵"Be careful," Jesus warned them. "Watch out for the yeast of the Pharisees and that of Herod."

¹⁶They discussed this with one another and

said, "It is because we have no bread." [17]Aware of their discussion, Jesus asked them: "Why are you talking about having no bread? Do you still not see or understand? Are your hearts hardened? [18]Do you have eyes but fail to see, and ears but fail to hear? And don't you remember? [19]When I broke the five loaves for the five thousand, how many basketfuls of pieces did you pick up?" "Twelve," they replied. [20]"And when I broke the seven loaves for the four thousand, how many basketfuls of pieces did you pick up?" They answered, "Seven." [21]He said to them, "Do you still not understand?"

Jesus invites those with ears to hear as well as enabling the blind to see. Here we have a story about a deaf man hearing, paralleled later by a blind man seeing (8.22–6). The spiritually blind and deaf are the cause of Jesus' passion in Mark. Jesus teaches the crowds, his disciples, scribes and Pharisees but many refuse to hear or see what he is about. By commanding this man to be opened he is calling on the nation to be open to his teaching. Sadly, even a repeat of the feeding miracle cuts no ice with the disciples who continue to be blind and deaf to the meaning. They neither have eyes that see nor ears that hear (8.18) that Jesus has power to deal with any situation. They need to recognize who Jesus is and what he represents. The evidence is before their eyes and ears.

- The Pharisees' demand for a sign is given short shrift (vv12–13). Why should Jesus perform a trick when already the blind see, the deaf hear, the hungry feed and the poor have the gospel preached to them?
- Can we believe the evidence of our eyes and ears?
- Are we open enough to see and hear what God has laid before us?
- Why is it that we remain resistant and obdurate to much of what the New Testament is saying?
- How is it that many outside the Church have a clearer picture of who Jesus is than those inside the Church?

PART 2

SECTION 5

OPEN TO THE TRUTH

21

Eyes Are Opened

Mark 8.22—9.1

²²**They came to Bethsaida, and some people** brought a blind man and begged Jesus to touch him. ²³He took the blind man by the hand and led him outside the village. When he had spat on the man's eyes and put his hands on him, Jesus asked, "Do you see anything?"

²⁴He looked up and said, "I see people; they look like trees walking around."

²⁵Once more Jesus put his hands on the man's eyes. Then his eyes were opened, his sight was restored, and he saw everything clearly. ²⁶Jesus sent him home, saying, "Don't go into the village."

²⁷Jesus and his disciples went on to the villages around Caesarea Philippi. On the way he asked them, "Who do people say I am?"

²⁸They replied, "Some say John the Baptist; others say Elijah; and still others, one of the prophets."

²⁹"But what about you?" he asked. "Who do you say I am?"

Peter answered, "You are the Christ."

³⁰Jesus warned them not to tell anyone about him.

³¹He then began to teach them that the Son of Man must suffer many things and be rejected by the elders, chief priests and teachers of the law, and that he must be killed and after three days rise again. ³²He spoke plainly about this, and Peter took him aside and began to rebuke him.

³³But when Jesus turned and looked at his disciples, he rebuked Peter. "Get behind me, Satan!" he said. "You do not have in mind the things of God, but the things of men."

³⁴Then he called the crowd to him along with his disciples and said: "If anyone would come after me, he must deny himself and take up his cross and follow me. ³⁵For whoever wants to save his life will lose it, but whoever loses his life for me and for the gospel will save it. ³⁶What good is it for a man to gain the whole world, yet forfeit his soul? ³⁷Or what can a man give in exchange for his soul? ³⁸If anyone is ashamed of me and my words in this adulterous and sinful generation, the Son of Man will be ashamed of him when he comes in his Father's glory with the holy angels."

⁹·¹And he said to them, "I tell you the truth, some who are standing here will not taste death before they see the kingdom of God come with power."

A deaf man was taken aside to be healed in 7.33; now a blind man is taken on one side for the same purpose. Luke and Matthew make no use of this story, but it is reminiscent of the much larger story in John 9 of the man born blind, slowly coming to faith. We are also reminded of the tale Mark will tell later of blind Bartimaeus in 10.46–52. Both men see clearly. The question is: Do the disciples also see?

Will the Caesarea Philippi incident provide them with an opportunity? This is often described as the watershed of Mark's Gospel – the great turning point in Jesus' relationship with his disciples. At last they see who he is, but we have to admit this is only momentary. And even when Peter, their spokesman, gets it right with 'You are the Christ' (v29), he immediately gets it very wrong (v33) so that Jesus has to rebuke him severely, calling him satanic!

The importance of the passage is that Jesus reveals to his disciples the meaning of his mission which will take him from here to Jerusalem and death. His journey to death and resurrection is linked to their role as disciples. They too are to take up their cross and follow him on his journey (v34). As we have seen, discipleship means following Jesus in the way of suffering and service.

- **Why did Jesus feel it necessary to suffer many things, be rejected and killed before he would rise up?**

- **Why should Jesus turn on Peter so vehemently?**

- **Who do people think Jesus is? Are they interested?**

- **Who do we say he is? Do we understand?**

- **Are we willing and able to take up our cross and follow him?**

22

Glory Displayed

Mark 9.2–13

²**After six days Jesus took Peter, James and** John with him and led them up a high mountain, where they were all alone. There he was transfigured before them. ³His clothes became dazzling white, whiter than anyone in the world could bleach them. ⁴And there appeared before them Elijah and Moses, who were talking with Jesus.

⁵Peter said to Jesus, "Rabbi, it is good for us to be here. Let us put up three shelters - one for you, one for Moses and one for Elijah." ⁶(He did not know what to say, they were so frightened.)

⁷Then a cloud appeared and enveloped them, and a voice came from the cloud: "This is my Son, whom I love. Listen to him!"

⁸Suddenly, when they looked round, they no longer saw anyone with them except Jesus. ⁹As they were coming down the mountain, Jesus gave them orders not to tell anyone what they had seen until the Son of Man had risen from the dead. ¹⁰They kept the matter to themselves, discussing what "rising from the dead" meant.

¹¹And they asked him, "Why do the teachers of the law say that Elijah must come first?" ¹²Jesus replied, "To be sure, Elijah does come first, and restores all things. Why then is it written that the Son of Man must suffer much and be rejected? ¹³But I tell you, Elijah has come, and they have done to him everything they wished, just as it is written about him."

Instead of Mark's usual connecting phrase, 'and immediately', we are given a six-day interlude between this incident and the confession of faith at Caesarea Philippi. Such a time span would give the disciples ample time to travel either to Mount Tabor or to the heights of Hermon. (Mark does not name the very high mountain). Today, Tabor marks the transfiguration site, and many pilgrims take the tortuous, hairpin ride to the top to meditate on this puzzling story. Mark emphasizes the whiteness of Jesus' clothes but tells us nothing of the discussion between Jesus and the two representatives of the law and the prophets, Moses and Elijah. We have seen that Mark is keen to present Jesus as the successor to these great figures of the past.

Peter recognizes that this is a significant moment and blurts out a silly remark about erecting tents (v5) possibly as a reference to the feast of tabernacles when the Jews remembered their wanderings with Moses in the wilderness. His answer comes from the awesome cloud of God's presence, and in the commission to listen to the 'beloved Son' who stands alone as the others fade (v8). Again Jesus is reticent about overexposure. The disciples are to tell no one until after the resurrection (v9). The theme of obtuseness is also present as they discuss what this can mean. Jesus reminds them that both the Son of Man and Elijah are treated with contempt.

- How is it that prophetic people like Moses, Elijah and Jesus are often treated with contempt or misunderstood?

- Do we need to find a 'high mountain', a place set apart, in order to perceive things differently?

- Are we able to witness a transfiguration in people as they come to understand their calling more fully?

- Are we ready to be changed in such a way?

- Is God asking us to listen to his Son?

23

'Have Pity on Us and Help Us'

Mark 9.14–29

¹⁴**When they came to the other disciples,** they saw a large crowd around them and the teachers of the law arguing with them. ¹⁵As soon as all the people saw Jesus, they were overwhelmed with wonder and ran to greet him.

¹⁶"What are you arguing with them about?" he asked.

¹⁷A man in the crowd answered, "Teacher, I brought you my son, who is possessed by a spirit that has robbed him of speech. ¹⁸Whenever it seizes him, it throws him to the ground. He foams at the mouth, gnashes his teeth and becomes rigid. I asked your disciples to drive out the spirit, but they could not."

¹⁹"O unbelieving generation," Jesus replied, "how long shall I stay with you? How long shall I put up with you? Bring the boy to me."

²⁰So they brought him. When the spirit saw Jesus, it immediately threw the boy into a convulsion. He fell to the ground and rolled around, foaming at the mouth.

²¹Jesus asked the boy's father, "How long has he been like this?"

"From childhood," he answered. ²²"It has often thrown him into fire or water to kill him. But if you can do anything, take pity on us and help us."

²³"'If you can'?" said Jesus. "Everything is possible for him who believes."

²⁴Immediately the boy's father exclaimed, "I do believe; help me overcome my unbelief!"

²⁵When Jesus saw that a crowd was running to the scene, he rebuked the evil spirit. "You deaf and mute spirit," he said, "I command you, come out of him and never enter him again."

²⁶The spirit shrieked, convulsed him violently and came out. The boy looked so much like a corpse that many said, "He's dead." ²⁷But Jesus took him by the hand and lifted him to his feet, and he stood up.

²⁸After Jesus had gone indoors, his disciples asked him privately, "Why couldn't we drive it out?"

²⁹He replied, "This kind can come out only by prayer."

Raphael's last great painting unites this scene with the transfiguration story. In the painting Jesus is displayed in dazzling white on the hilltop flanked by Moses and Elijah, while below, the disciples struggle to heal an epileptic boy. The painting marks the contrast between the serenity of the mountain top and the chaos and confusion below. This is well reflected in Mark's text. The crowds run about (v15, v25) and there is an argument (v14). Jesus shows his exasperation when he discovers the impotence of the disciples (v19).

As in life there are a series of peaks and troughs. The father of the afflicted boy is obviously at his wit's end and pleads, 'If you can do anything, take pity on us' (v22). This provokes more anger from Jesus who calls on the man to display some semblance of faith – to which the poor father exclaims, 'I do believe; help me overcome my unbelief!' (v24). We can all sympathize. The man's honesty and direct appeal provoke Jesus to undertake the exorcism.

Perhaps we, like the disciples, can admit to being troubled by this story (v28). For Mark, the story has to do with building up faith. It is well known that the early Christians were fearful (16.8) and here Jesus condemns them for being faithless (v19). But if they can cry out *'Kyrie eleison'* (Lord have mercy) then there will be a response.

- **Does this story echo our own experiences? How do we react in a crisis when our faith is put to the test?**

- **Why were the disciples unable to help? Were they too encountering a crisis of faith?**

- **What is the role of the crowd in this scene? Notice how the passage begins with them marvelling at Jesus rather than ending with the usual expression of amazement. Is there something about Jesus and his appearance that they recognize and to which they respond? Remember how Moses looked when he came down the mountain (Exod. 34.30).**

- **Why is it that this kind of exorcism can only be achieved by prayer (v29)?**

- **What is exorcism?**

- **How do we understand such healings today?**

24

On Achieving True Greatness in the Kingdom

Mark 9.30–50

³⁰**They left that place and passed through** Galilee. Jesus did not want anyone to know where they were, ³¹because he was teaching his disciples. He said to them, "The Son of Man is going to be betrayed into the hands of men. They will kill him, and after three days he will rise." ³²But they did not understand what he meant and were afraid to ask him about it.

³³They came to Capernaum. When he was in the house, he asked them, "What were you arguing about on the road?" ³⁴But they kept quiet because on the way they had argued about who was the greatest.

³⁵Sitting down, Jesus called the Twelve and said, "If anyone wants to be first, he must be the very last, and the servant of all."

³⁶He took a little child and had him stand among them. Taking him in his arms, he said to them, ³⁷"Whoever welcomes one of these little children in my name welcomes me; and whoever welcomes me does not welcome me but the one who sent me."

³⁸"Teacher," said John, "we saw a man driving out demons in your name and we told him to stop, because he was not one of us."

³⁹"Do not stop him," Jesus said. "No-one who does a miracle in my name can in the next moment say anything bad about me, ⁴⁰for whoever is not against us is for us. ⁴¹I tell you the truth, anyone who gives you a cup of water in my name because you belong to Christ will certainly not lose his reward.

⁴²"And if anyone causes one of these little ones who believe in me to sin, it would be better for him to be thrown into the sea with a large millstone tied around his neck. ⁴³If your hand causes you to sin, cut it off. It is better for you to enter life maimed than with two hands to go into hell, where the fire never goes out, ⁴⁴[where, "'their worm does not die, and the fire is not quenched.'] ⁴⁵And if your foot causes you to sin, cut it off. It is better for you to enter life crippled than to have two feet and be thrown into hell, ⁴⁶[where, "'their worm does not die, and the fire is not quenched.'] ⁴⁷And if your eye causes you to sin, pluck it out. It is better for you to enter the kingdom of God with one eye than to have two eyes and be thrown into hell, ⁴⁸where

"'their worm does not die, and the fire is not quenched.' ⁴⁹Everyone will be salted with fire. ⁵⁰"Salt is good, but if it loses its saltiness, how can you make it salty again? Have salt in yourselves, and be at peace with each other."

Again there is the note of secrecy (v30). This time the reason given is that Jesus is instructing his disciples. Indeed, in this second half of the Gospel the central emphasis moves from public to more private teaching as the theme of discipleship is developed.

The first condition of being a disciple is to understand who the master is and where he is leading. The answer is given in this second passion prediction (v31). Sadly the disciples fail to understand and, even worse, are too fearful to ask Jesus what he means.

The fact that they are pig-headed is suggested in the following passage which reveals that while Jesus has been teaching them about discipleship they have been arguing about who is the greatest (v34). Such childish behaviour is exposed by Jesus setting a child in front of them and commending childlike trust rather than infantile arguments about status. This is one of the most tender scenes in the Gospels, when Jesus puts his arms around a child. Anyone who receives the weak and vulnerable receives Christ himself (v37). This has no effect on the disciples who continue to want to exclude outsiders (v38). Children are models of faithful trusting disciples and must not be offended.

The theme of offence continues with hyperbolic sayings about chopping off hands and feet (vv43–4). Jesus uses exaggerated language to emphasize the value of life. Separation from God does not compare with the loss of a limb. Those prepared to suffer loss will be rewarded with life (compare 8.34, 38). The disciple must prove himself in this respect and not lose the saltiness that marks him out as a follower of Jesus (v50).

- **How salty are we? (Dead Sea 'salt' could lose its flavour if the salt content were washed out of the white salty deposit.)**

- **Can we be relied on to remain faithful disciples even in the face of loss and disaster?**

- **Do we give children a central place in our Christian community?**

- **Do they get in the way or should we see them as leading the way to a trusting, mature relationship?**

25

Family Matters and the Kingdom

Mark 10.1–16

¹**Jesus then left that place and went into the region of Judea and across the Jordan. Again crowds of people came to him, and as was his custom, he taught them.**
²Some Pharisees came and tested him by asking, "Is it lawful for a man to divorce his wife?"
³"What did Moses command you?" he replied. ⁴They said, "Moses permitted a man to write a certificate of divorce and send her away."
⁵"It was because your hearts were hard that Moses wrote you this law," Jesus replied. ⁶"But at the beginning of creation God 'made them male and female'. ⁷'For this reason a man will leave his father and mother and be united to his wife, ⁸and the two will become one flesh.' So they are no longer two, but one. ⁹Therefore what God has joined together, let man not separate."
¹⁰When they were in the house again, the disciples asked Jesus about this. ¹¹He answered, "Anyone who divorces his wife and marries another woman commits adultery against her. ¹²And if she divorces her husband and marries another man, she commits adultery."
¹³People were bringing little children to Jesus to have him touch them, but the disciples rebuked them. ¹⁴When Jesus saw this, he was indignant. He said to them, "Let the little children come to me, and do not hinder them, for the kingdom of God belongs to such as these. ¹⁵I tell you the truth, anyone who will not receive the kingdom of God like a little child will never enter it." ¹⁶And he took the children in his arms, put his hands on them and blessed them.

As before, Jesus is seen to be in conflict with the current interpretation of Mosaic law. The issue arises out of a debate in which the Pharisees try to trap Jesus (v2). Jesus is seen here to be the one who fully understands God's will behind the law on divorce which Moses has added as a concession. It is well known that at the time of Jesus the rabbis hotly debated the grounds for divorce. For some, a woman could be sent packing for burning a man's dinner. For others, only if she had committed adultery.

Jesus is seen to make radical demands. He points to what God intended marriage to mean: 'the two become one flesh' (v7). A new creation takes place – the two become one. In some ways this is what the gospel is all about – marriage is the icon of the union between God and humanity, heaven and earth, male and female, slave and free, Jew and Gentile – all are one in Christ.

The claims of discipleship are more rigorous than the law of Moses. The time for a new beginning is here, when men treat their women with respect and equality, not as goods and chattels to be cast off at whim. Divorce is only necessary because of human failure. Jesus is pointing to the ideal set out for all at creation. To simplify the issue the text turns to the centrality of children. It is a reminder that the kingdom of God is given as a gift to those who have the grace and trust to receive it. Here is a warning to those in the community who try to claim the kingdom for themselves or, even worse, try to exclude others – in this case the weak and vulnerable.

- Is divorce forbidden for Christians, and lifelong marriage a command rather than an ideal at which we should aim?

- If divorce is forbidden, what has happened to the gospel of forgiveness?

- Is our present situation of easy divorce akin to the first century situation Jesus was addressing?

- How can we sustain and help married people?

- Are we guilty of trying to prevent the young from getting to Jesus?

SECTION 6

OPEN TO DISCIPLESHIP

26

Riches and the Kingdom

Mark 10.17–31

¹⁷**As Jesus started on his way, a man ran up** to him and fell on his knees before him. "Good teacher," he asked, "what must I do to inherit eternal life?"

¹⁸"Why do you call me good?" Jesus answered. "No-one is good - except God alone. ¹⁹You know the commandments: 'Do not murder, do not commit adultery, do not steal, do not give false testimony, do not defraud, honour your father and mother.'"

²⁰"Teacher," he declared, "all these I have kept since I was a boy."

²¹Jesus looked at him and loved him. "One thing you lack," he said. "Go, sell everything you have and give to the poor, and you will have treasure in heaven. Then come, follow me."

²²At this the man's face fell. He went away sad, because he had great wealth.

²³Jesus looked around and said to his disciples, "How hard it is for the rich to enter the kingdom of God!"

²⁴The disciples were amazed at his words. But Jesus said again, "Children, how hard it is to enter the kingdom of God! ²⁵It is easier for a camel to go through the eye of a needle than for a rich man to enter the kingdom of God."

²⁶The disciples were even more amazed, and said to each other, "Who then can be saved?"

²⁷Jesus looked at them and said, "With man this is impossible, but not with God; all things are possible with God."

²⁸Peter said to him, "We have left everything to follow you!"

²⁹"I tell you the truth," Jesus replied, "no-one who has left home or brothers or sisters or mother or father or children or fields for me and the gospel ³⁰will fail to receive a hundred times as much in this present age (homes, brothers, sisters, mothers, children and fields - and with them, persecutions) and in the age to come, eternal life. ³¹But many who are first will be last, and the last first."

One of the things a disciple must renounce in pursuit of the kingdom is the inordinate love of riches. We have seen how the worries of this world and the lures of riches distract them from growing to maturity in the kingdom of God (4.19). A practical example is set before us in this story of the rich young man. Rembrandt's most famous etching, *The Hundred Guilder Print*, displays this by showing the young man staring into space, frozen and unable to respond to Jesus' call to discipleship. This is in marked contrast to his enthusiastic running up to Jesus, eager to find the key to eternal life (v17). No wonder Jesus loved him for it (v21). The steady gaze of Christ penetrates the man's weakness. He cannot renounce his great wealth, his main preoccupation. Discipleship is about putting the kingdom first.

The incident is used for a private seminar with the disciples on the dangers of riches. Like many of their contemporaries, the disciples believed riches were an indication of God's pleasure and reward for good conduct. For Jesus, it is the poor who are closer to God. The disciples, almost unknowingly, have in fact followed this path and left everything to follow Jesus (v28). Renouncing family ties for the sake of the gospel has its own rewards (v30). After all, has not Jesus broken with his earthly family over this very issue? (3.31–5).

- **Does this passage exclude the rich from God's kingdom?**

- **How can we help those distracted by wealth to cultivate a different attitude towards possessions?**

- **Is the Church too preoccupied with its financial and material investments to notice what is being said in this passage?**

- **What radical demands are being made of us?**

- **How seriously do we take the saying (often repeated in the Gospels) about the first being last, and the last first (v31)?**

27

Jesus Predicts His Passion for the Third Time

Mark 10.32–4

³²**They were on their way up to Jerusalem, with Jesus leading the way, and the disciples were astonished, while those who followed were afraid. Again he took the Twelve aside and told them what was going to happen to him.** ³³**"We are going up to Jerusalem,"** he said, **"and the Son of Man will be betrayed to the chief priests and teachers of the law. They will condemn him to death and will hand him over to the Gentiles,** ³⁴**who will mock him and spit on him, flog him and kill him. Three days later he will rise."**

Mark reminds us that Jesus and his disciples are 'on their way up to Jerusalem' (v32). There is purpose and direction in all that Jesus undertakes, and the disciples must learn what following Jesus will involve.

This third and final passion prediction fully describes what will happen in some detail. Like the tolling of a great bell foretelling the inevitable, these predictions have come at regular intervals ever since the turning point of Caesarea Philippi (8.31, 9.31 and here). Notice how Jesus talks about his being handed over (v33); this is a necessary part of God's plan (8.31). Resurrection can only be achieved by Jesus willingly taking up his cross.

The disciples are 'astonished' and 'afraid' (v32). The same Greek word is used in the Garden of Gethsemane narrative. It indicates the horror they all feel at the thought of what walking up to Jerusalem will lead to. Mark is again stressing the discipleship theme. Before Christians were ever known as Christians, they were described as followers in the 'Way' (Acts 9.2). This Way (*hodos* in Greek) leads to death and glory. It is significant that all the passion predictions are made while the disciples are on the road (*hodos* – the same Greek word).

- Some critics think the passion predictions are read back into the text, with the benefit of hindsight. Do you think Jesus could have foreseen what would happen to him?

- Was it not obvious to anyone with political insight that this 'new teaching' which Jesus represented would end in a showdown with the establishment?

- Are we fearful of and horrified by the demands of discipleship? Where is this gospel leading us? Are we prepared to follow?

28

The Cost of Discipleship

Mark 10.35–45

³⁵Then James and John, the sons of Zebedee, came to him. "Teacher," they said, "we want you to do for us whatever we ask."
³⁶"What do you want me to do for you?" he asked.
³⁷They replied, "Let one of us sit at your right and the other at your left in your glory."
³⁸"You don't know what you are asking," Jesus said. "Can you drink the cup I drink or be baptised with the baptism I am baptised with?"
³⁹"We can," they answered.
Jesus said to them, "You will drink the cup I drink and be baptised with the baptism I am baptised with, ⁴⁰but to sit at my right or left is not for me to grant. These places belong to those for whom they have been prepared."
⁴¹When the ten heard about this, they became indignant with James and John. ⁴²Jesus called them together and said, "You know that those who are regarded as rulers of the Gentiles lord it over them, and their high officials exercise authority over them. ⁴³Not so with you. Instead, whoever wants to become great among you must be your servant, ⁴⁴and whoever wants to be first must be slave of all. ⁴⁵For even the Son of Man did not come to be served, but to serve, and to give his life as a ransom for many."

Mark cruelly casts the disciples in the most crass mould. As with the second passion prediction, we are told a story of the disciples' failure to understand what Jesus is saying and its implication for their own lives. Another argument has arisen about greatness. James and John want the best seats in the kingdom (v37). They see leadership in terms of status and privilege. However, Jesus is among them as one who serves (v45). He does not exercise an overbearing domination even though he is among them as a 'Teacher' (v35). The lesson he has to teach is about service and self-effacement.

Little do James and John understand that the only throne Jesus will mount will be a wooden one, that the only crown he will receive is that of thorns, and that those who will be at his right and left will be crucified thieves. The baptism they are offered is to be buried and rise again with Christ. The cup he offers is one of suffering. Here we have the most direct link yet between baptism, discipleship and suffering.

No wonder the ten are indignant with James and John. They need to learn the lesson that 'whoever wants to be first must be slave to all' (v44).

The final verse of this section introduces a new idea which interprets Jesus' sacrifice in terms of a 'ransom for many'. Jesus will save many by dying and setting an example of selfless giving which the disciples must copy. Such a display of sacrificial love will inspire many to take up their cross and follow him.

- Do we exhibit the same crass, self-seeking as James and John?
- Are people indignant with a Church that so often fails to practise what it preaches?
- What do the sacraments of baptism and Holy Communion say about discipleship?
- In what sense is Jesus' death a ransom for many?

29

A Blind Man Sees
the Way to Follow Jesus

Mark 10.46–52

⁴⁶**Then they came to Jericho. As Jesus and** his disciples, together with a large crowd, were leaving the city, a blind man, Bartimaeus (that is, the Son of Timaeus), was sitting by the roadside begging. ⁴⁷When he heard that it was Jesus of Nazareth, he began to shout, "Jesus, Son of David, have mercy on me!" ⁴⁸Many rebuked him and told him to be quiet, but he shouted all the more, "Son of David, have mercy on me!" ⁴⁹Jesus stopped and said, "Call him."

So they called to the blind man, "Cheer up! On your feet! He's calling you." ⁵⁰Throwing his cloak aside, he jumped to his feet and came to Jesus. ⁵¹"What do you want me to do for you?" Jesus asked him. The blind man said, "Rabbi, I want to see." ⁵²"Go," said Jesus, "your faith has healed you." Immediately he received his sight and followed Jesus along the road.

This is a remarkable story, full of irony and insight. Jesus has been teaching his followers about discipleship. He has done this 'plainly' (8.32). Sadly, they remain largely blind and deaf. Now at the very door of Jerusalem, a blind man sits beside the way and cries out *'Christe eleison'* – 'Jesus, have mercy on me' (v47). The oldest prayer in Christendom is found on the lips of this blind beggar who recognizes Jesus' true messianic status as 'Son of David' (v47). Blind? He sees more clearly than any of the disciples! He is told to be silent and restrained like the mothers with their children (10.13). But nothing can silence this man who knows his need and is fearless to express it. He shouts louder (v48). Jesus stops and gives instructions that Bartimaeus be brought. The bystanders now change their tune and offer encouragement. Bartimaeus behaves like the model disciple throwing off his cloak, the symbol of begging. He jumps up and comes to Jesus. We are reminded that the calling of a disciple is to be with Jesus (3.14). He makes his request known by addressing Jesus as *Rabbuni* (Rabbi) (v51) – the same word Mary Magdalene used of Jesus in the

Easter garden (John 20.16). This faith has 'saved' Bartimaeus. He sees well enough to be a follower in the Way (v52).

- What is Mark telling us in this story about a blind man seeing more clearly than the twelve disciples?

- How clearly can we see? Read George Herbert's hymn, 'Teach me my God and king'.

- Do the crowd represent the common convention of 'Don't bother religious leaders - they are too busy to be interested'?

- How much noise are we prepared to make to get ourselves noticed? Are we easily put down? If so, can we take encouragement from Bartimaeus?

30

The Triumphal Entry into Jerusalem

Mark 11.1–11

¹**As they approached Jerusalem and came** to Bethphage and Bethany at the Mount of Olives, Jesus sent two of his disciples, ²saying to them, "Go to the village ahead of you, and just as you enter it, you will find a colt tied there, which no-one has ever ridden. Untie it and bring it here. ³If anyone asks you, 'Why are you doing this?' tell him, 'The Lord needs it and will send it back here shortly.'"
⁴They went and found a colt outside in the street, tied at a doorway. As they untied it, ⁵some people standing there asked, "What are you doing, untying that colt?" ⁶They answered as Jesus had told them to, and the people let them go. ⁷When they brought the colt to Jesus and threw their cloaks over it, he sat on it. ⁸Many people spread their cloaks on the road, while others spread branches they had cut in the fields. ⁹Those who went ahead and those who followed shouted,

"Hosanna!"

"Blessed is he who comes in the name of the Lord!"

¹⁰"Blessed is the coming kingdom of our father David!"

"Hosanna in the highest!"

¹¹Jesus entered Jerusalem and went to the temple. He looked around at everything, but since it was already late, he went out to Bethany with the Twelve.

Here we have a passage which rings with intrigue. Obviously, Jesus has contacts in and around Jerusalem who will help him put into effect a pre-arranged plan. Passwords are exchanged; a colt, the means of entry, is secured; and a small quasi-messianic demonstration is put into effect. The scene is set for a triumphal entry – an opportunity for Israel and its leaders to recognize who Jesus is and what he represents. We remember that this is the main purpose for Mark writing this Gospel. Sadly, as the story unfolds, both Israel and her leaders reject Jesus, seeing him as a messianic pretender guilty of blasphemy. Here at least a number of people take up the cry of 'Hosanna', but Mark does not say whether those who cry are calling down blessings on the pilgrims entering Jerusalem or acclaiming Jesus.

It seems odd that if this incident was understood as a messianic claim, no mention of it was made at the trial of Jesus. The fact that Jesus rides a 'colt' is not necessarily a mark of humility; it was an appropriate mount for a king in the ancient world. To walk would have been more humble but then the entry would not have been remarkable. Mark is perhaps alluding to Zechariah 9.9 and noting that those who have the eyes of faith will see what they need to see in these events.

The episode ends on a downbeat note. Jesus enters the Temple, merely looks around and returns to the encampment at Bethany. Mark again intrigues us by having his characters not fully understand the events in which they are caught up. After the resurrection things will become clearer.

- The fickle crowd cry 'Hosanna' and afford Jesus a welcome but within days they will have turned against him. How fickle is our faith? Do we say one thing while believing another?

- How overt is this as a messianic demonstration? Is Jesus laying claim to kingship?

- How do we expect our leaders to behave in public?

- How do we rate humility in such circumstances?

SECTION 7

OPEN TO THE CHALLENGE

31

Cursing a Fig Tree
and Cleansing the Temple

Mark 11.12–26

¹²**The next day as they were leaving Bethany,** Jesus was hungry. ¹³Seeing in the distance a fig-tree in leaf, he went to find out if it had any fruit. When he reached it, he found nothing but leaves, because it was not the season for figs. ¹⁴ Then he said to the tree, "May no-one ever eat fruit from you again." And his disciples heard him say it.

¹⁵On reaching Jerusalem, Jesus entered the temple area and began driving out those who were buying and selling there. He overturned the tables of the money changers and the benches of those selling doves, ¹⁶and would not allow anyone to carry merchandise through the temple courts. ¹⁷And as he taught them, he said, "Is it not written:

"'My house will be called a house of prayer for all nations'?

But you have made it 'a den of robbers'."

¹⁸The chief priests and the teachers of the law heard this and began looking for a way to kill him, for they feared him, because the whole crowd was amazed at his teaching.

¹⁹When evening came, they went out of the city.

²⁰In the morning, as they went along, they saw the fig-tree withered from the roots. ²¹Peter remembered and said to Jesus, "Rabbi, look! The fig-tree you cursed has withered!"

²²"Have faith in God," Jesus answered. ²³"I tell you the truth, if anyone says to this mountain, 'Go, throw yourself into the sea,' and does not doubt in his heart but believes that what he says will happen, it will be done for him. ²⁴Therefore I tell you, whatever you ask for in prayer, believe that you have received it, and it will be yours. ²⁵And when you stand praying, if you hold anything against anyone, forgive him, so that your Father in heaven may forgive you your sins. ²⁶[But if you do not forgive, neither will your Father who is in heaven forgive your sins.]"

Mark provides us with another sandwich. The fig tree story tops and tails this passage so that both themes are seen to be intertwined. The fig tree was seen as a symbol of Israel, the Temple was the nation's ritual heart. In this section both are seen to be dried up, corrupt and utterly barren. Instead of blossoming and fruiting at the dawning of the messianic age, the fig tree is found to be nothing but leaf (v13). Like Israel, the fig tree is unable to deliver. At the appointed time it was exposed as an empty sham. The Temple too had forgotten its original purpose. No longer was it a 'house of prayer for all nations' (Isa. 56.7); now it had become 'a den of robbers' (Jer. 7.11). Both these texts are found in v17. Mark is the only Evangelist to put these two texts together. He understood what the Temple should have been and recognized what it had become. Here he shows Jesus exposing the sham as did Jeremiah before him.

This is a difficult passage for many of us. It reveals Jesus in an alien light – ill-tempered with a fig tree and angry with small-time traders. We have to remember Mark's purpose is to present Jesus in conflict with the Jewish authorities who attempt to destroy him for exposing their impotence. In Mark's scheme, God is rejecting Israel because she has failed to recognize her Messiah. Not only has Israel failed in this regard, she has not achieved her mission to draw all nations to the worship of God. The tawdry sale of animals and the exchange of coinage had made it impossible for God-fearing Gentiles to worship in the Temple confines. Had Israel been faithful and prayerful then things might have been different (vv23–5). Notice how v25 makes an oblique reference to the clause in the Lord's prayer about forgiveness.

- **How much sham is there in the practice of our religion?**

- **Do we need to take a whip hand to all that clutters up our life?**

- **Has the clatter of our gaining and getting made us deaf to the voice of God?**

- **How firm is our faith? Do we have 'no doubt in our hearts'? (v23).**

- **Notice the centrality of forgiveness (v25). Do we limit God's forgiveness with our hardness of heart?**

32

The Authority of Jesus
Is Put to the Question

Mark 11.27–33

²⁷**They arrived again in Jerusalem, and while** Jesus was walking in the temple courts, the chief priests, the teachers of the law and the elders came to him. ²⁸"By what authority are you doing these things?" they asked. "And who gave you authority to do this?" ²⁹Jesus replied, "I will ask you one question. Answer me, and I will tell you by what authority I am doing these things. ³⁰John's baptism - was it from heaven, or from men? Tell me!"

³¹They discussed it among themselves and said, "If we say, 'From heaven', he will ask, 'Then why didn't you believe him?' ³²But if we say, 'From men'. . . ." (They feared the people, for everyone held that John really was a prophet.)

³³So they answered Jesus, "We don't know." Jesus said, "Neither will I tell you by what authority I am doing these things."

The central questions in Mark have been 'Who is Jesus?', 'What is his authority?' In chapter 1 it made a deep impression on the crowds that, 'unlike the scribes, he taught with authority'. Now this authority is under question (v28). All the religious leaders have come together to challenge him as some of them did in 3.22–30. Had they understood the meaning of these events – the triumphal entry, the cleansing of the Temple, etc. – they would have had no need to ask this question.

Jesus cleverly turns the question on to the interrogators. He exposes their political machinations and desperate need to curry favour with the people (v32). In so doing, Jesus links the source of his authority with that of John the Baptist, who by now is being revered as a martyr–prophet. The avoidance of acknowledging this truth is exposed by Jesus' question. They, like the fig tree, are impotent and barren. Jesus refuses to answer their question as they refuse to answer his. In reality the answer is obvious as it was to the crowds in chapter 1 – but there are always some who will stubbornly refuse to accept the truth.

Interestingly, the discussion turns on the validity of John's baptism (v30). Obviously, the religious leaders were suspicious of John and his baptisms. Mark is suggesting the reason is because baptism is a sign of repentance – a turning about (*metanoia* in the Greek, 1.4). These Jewish leaders have no intention of changing their ways and accepting the new self-authenticating authority which Jesus represents. Those who follow Jesus and acknowledge his authority must submit to baptism and drink the cup of suffering and self-emptying (10.38).

- Is there part of us which obstinately refuses to acknowledge the truth?

- What is it in human nature which perversely paints black as white and white as black?

- Are our politicians guilty of manipulating the truth? Do they constantly seek to appease and curry favour?

- Where is the centre of authority in our lives?

33

A Parable about Rejection

Mark 12.1–12

¹**He then began to speak to them in parables:** "A man planted a vineyard. He put a wall around it, dug a pit for the winepress and built a watchtower. Then he rented the vineyard to some farmers and went away on a journey. ²At harvest time he sent a servant to the tenants to collect from them some of the fruit of the vineyard. ³But they seized him, beat him and sent him away empty-handed. ⁴Then he sent another servant to them; they struck this man on the head and treated him shamefully. ⁵He sent still another, and that one they killed. He sent many others; some of them they beat, others they killed.

⁶"He had one left to send, a son, whom he loved. He sent him last of all, saying, `They will respect my son.'

⁷"But the tenants said to one another, 'This is the heir. Come, let's kill him, and the inheritance will be ours.' ⁸So they took him and killed him, and threw him out of the vineyard.

⁹"What then will the owner of the vineyard do? He will come and kill those tenants and give the vineyard to others. ¹⁰Haven't you read this scripture:

"'The stone the builders rejected has become the capstone;

¹¹the Lord has done this, and it is marvellous in our eyes'?"

¹²Then they looked for a way to arrest him because they knew he had spoken the parable against them. But they were afraid of the crowd; so they left him and went away.

The whole of this chapter is set in the Temple precincts. Here Jesus is caught in a web of tension and conflict which will culminate in his prophecy of doom for that building (13.1–2), one of the wonders of the ancient world. In this passage Jesus tells a parable which is more like an allegory than any other. It is impossible not to conclude that the villains are the religious leaders. Indeed they come to this very conclusion themselves (v12) and would have liked to arrest Jesus, but are unable to do so because of Jesus' popularity with the crowds.

What we have to examine in this section is what this parable reveals about Mark's understanding of Jesus. We have to conclude that Mark is convinced of Jesus' messianic identity (1.1). He also sees Jesus as part of a long line of prophets all of which had tried to warn Israel and recall them back to God. We cannot help ask the question, 'Is this how Jesus saw himself?' What is certain from this passage is that the nation is indicted for not producing fruit (as in the story of the fig tree). Those who reject God's message will themselves be rejected.

The fact that the story speaks nothing of the resurrection but only promises the rejection and death of the emissaries from God is puzzling. But vv10–11 do allude to Jesus' eventual vindication, and were used as a popular proof text by early Christians.

- How much warning do we need before we recognize the need to be responsive and fruitful?

- How responsive are our religious leaders to God's messengers and prophets?

- Who are today's prophets? Are they recognized? Do they speak out fearlessly?

- Is it inevitable that an institution will learn to forget the rock from which it was hewn?

- Can you cite a case of an idea or teaching that was once rejected and which now has become central?

34

Trick Questions

Mark.12.13–27

¹³**Later they sent some of the Pharisees and Herodians to Jesus to catch him in his words.** ¹⁴They came to him and said, "Teacher, we know you are a man of integrity. You aren't swayed by men, because you pay no attention to who they are; but you teach the way of God in accordance with the truth. Is it right to pay taxes to Caesar or not? ¹⁵Should we pay or shouldn't we?"

But Jesus knew their hypocrisy. "Why are you trying to trap me?" he asked. "Bring me a denarius and let me look at it." ¹⁶They brought the coin, and he asked them, "Whose portrait is this? And whose inscription?"

"Caesar's," they replied.

¹⁷Then Jesus said to them, "Give to Caesar what is Caesar's and to God what is God's." And they were amazed at him.

¹⁸Then the Sadducees, who say there is no resurrection, came to him with a question. ¹⁹"Teacher," they said, "Moses wrote for us that if a man's brother dies and leaves a wife but no children, the man must marry the widow and have children for his brother. ²⁰Now there were seven brothers. The first one married and died without leaving any children. ²¹The second one married the widow, but he also died, leaving no child. It was the same with the third. ²²In fact, none of the seven left any children. Last of all, the woman died too. ²³At the resurrection whose wife will she be, since the seven were married to her?"

²⁴Jesus replied, "Are you not in error because you do not know the Scriptures or the power of God? ²⁵When the dead rise, they will neither marry nor be given in marriage; they will be like the angels in heaven. ²⁶Now about the dead rising - have you not read in the book of Moses, in the account of the bush, how God said to him, 'I am the God of Abraham, the God of Isaac, and the God of Jacob'? ²⁷He is not the God of the dead, but of the living. You are badly mistaken!"

Two questions are directed at Jesus by two different power groups. They are both intended to trap Jesus and be used as evidence of his political and doctrinal defects. It is interesting to notice how Jesus handles this sort of tactic. Can you detect the use of humour in his replies?

The first question comes from the Pharisees and Herodians, who were first grouped together in 3.6 plotting to destroy Jesus. Now that Jesus has come to the power centre of Jerusalem, they can attempt to put their resolve into practice. They do so by asking a question not unlike the question, 'Have you stopped beating your wife?' If he suggests not paying taxes then he will be in trouble with the Roman authorities. If he advocates taxation then many of his followers will be dismayed. Mark indicates that Jesus is fully aware of the malice behind this question (v15) and invites his questioners to hand him a coin. They do so and immediately his adversaries are exposed as guilty of using Roman currency with its graven imagery. His reply invites us to be adult and responsible in differentiating what belongs to God and what is our political responsibility. If Jesus is suggesting that there is nothing that does not belong to God, no wonder his questioners are taken off their guard (v17).

The second question comes from the Sadducees. These, unlike the Pharisees, represent a conservative, priestly faction in Judaism. They have no belief in the newfangled doctrine of resurrection and seek to expose its inadequacy by telling a silly story. Jesus upbraids them for their inept understanding both of Scripture and the risen life. As he points out, even according to the 'book of Moses' (v26) – the only authority the Sadducees recognize – there is evidence of a continuous life after death as evidenced in the story of the burning bush. Far from being fazed by their mockery and disbelief, Jesus is seen to be living proof of what the fourth Gospel calls the 'resurrection and the life' (John 11.25).

- How often do we try to ridicule or trap our opponents by setting this sort of trick question?

- When our politicians and media interviewers behave like this do we applaud or condemn?

- Is there a power group in our church or society which is bent on destroying new and creative initiatives? How do we handle such opposition – how useful is humour in this?

35

A Scribe Asks a Question

Mark 12.28–34

²⁸**One of the teachers of the law came and** heard them debating. Noticing that Jesus had given them a good answer, he asked him, "Of all the commandments, which is the most important?" ²⁹"The most important one," answered Jesus, "is this: 'Hear, O Israel, the Lord our God, the Lord is one. ³⁰Love the Lord your God with all your heart and with all your soul and with all your mind and with all your strength.' ³¹The second is this: 'Love your neighbour as yourself.' There is no commandment greater than these." ³²"Well said, teacher," the man replied. "You are right in saying that God is one and there is no other but him. ³³To love him with all your heart, with all your understanding and with all your strength, and to love your neighbour as yourself is more important than all burnt offerings and sacrifices." ³⁴When Jesus saw that he had answered wisely, he said to him, "You are not far from the kingdom of God." And from then on no-one dared ask him any more questions.

After Pharisees and Sadducees, we encounter a scribe with a burning question. This time the motive is not malicious but simply to get to the truth. As the Gospels are written with this question in mind we are meant to take note of the reply.

Before we examine what Jesus has to say, it is of interest to examine Mark's treatment of the scribe. Jesus commends his thoughtful response (v34) and as we have seen, the scribe is impressed with Jesus' debating powers (v28). When Matthew and Luke make use of this story, the scribe has reverted to type and is cast in the role of a villain setting a trap (Matt. 22.35; Luke 10.25). We have seen this stereotyping in Mark but this time the mould is broken and Jesus is in conversation with a friendly scribe.

It has to be said that there must have been a number of scribes and Pharisees well disposed to Jesus for the Christian movement to have spread so rapidly. Certainly Jesus seems to have been closer to Pharisees in outlook than to the more conservative Sadducees and scribes. If, later in the first century, disputes between Jews and Christians led to stereotyping, we can be sad but understand how these things happen.

Jesus replies to the enquiring scribe by quoting from the law of Moses. In so doing he reminds us that there is no conflict between the demands of God and the demands of the gospel. His summary of the law is one which the scribe would recognize and endorse. Indeed every good Jew repeats similar words every day in the form of the *'Shema'*. To make this a priority and to put it into practice remains the challenge of all those who 'are not far from the kingdom of God' (v34).

- **Does this passage suggest that there is more in common between Jews and Christians than we believe?**

- **Are we in danger of stereotyping people we do not understand?**

- **Are we ready to applaud when the truth is stated clearly and unequivocally? Would this encourage more plain speaking?**

- **How do we put this 'summary of the law' into practice when we hardly know our neighbour and have almost squeezed God out of our 'busy' lives?**

- **Is not tinkering with the liturgy a more attractive escape than the real issue (v33)?**

SECTION 8

OPEN TO DESTRUCTION

36

Jesus Asks a Question, Adds a Caution and Provides an Example

Mark 12.35–44

[35]**While Jesus was teaching in the temple courts, he asked, "How is it that the teachers of the law say that the Christ is the son of David?** [36]**David himself, speaking by the Holy Spirit, declared:**

"'The Lord said to my Lord: "Sit at my right hand until I put your enemies under your feet."'

[37]**David himself calls him 'Lord'. How then can he be his son?"**

The large crowd listened to him with delight. [38]**As he taught, Jesus said, "Watch out for the teachers of the law. They like to walk around in flowing robes and be greeted in the market-places,** [39]**and have the most important seats in the synagogues and the places of honour** at banquets. [40]**They devour widows' houses and for a show make lengthy prayers. Such men will be punished most severely."**

[41]**Jesus sat down opposite the place where the offerings were put and watched the crowd putting their money into the temple treasury. Many rich people threw in large amounts.** [42]**But a poor widow came and put in two very small copper coins, worth only a fraction of a penny.**

[43]**Calling his disciples to him, Jesus said, "I tell you the truth, this poor widow has put more into the treasury than all the others.** [44]**They all gave out of their wealth; but she, out of her poverty, put in everything - all she had to live on."**

If Jesus is the Messiah then he will be a 'son of David'. Matthew and Luke emphasize this by having Jesus born in Bethlehem, the city of David, and tracing his pedigree back to David (by two different routes). Mark has Jesus authoritatively confronting this issue head on. If there were disputes between Jews and Christians about whether or not Jesus was a son of David, then the best way of dealing with it is to present a Jesus who is superior to David and to whom David would defer. The Gospels are concerned to show that there is one they proclaim who is greater than Moses and David. As usual, Mark has the people responding to such clear speaking with 'delight' (v37). But if Jesus is of greater significance than David he does not look for the adulation that the official teachers seek. There is nothing more loathsome to the

Jesus of Mark than a parade of false piety. In condemning the hypocrisy of the scribes, Jesus is standing in the prophetic tradition. There are echoes here of Malachi's condemnation of those who oppress the widow (Mal. 3.5).

The widow herself appears in the final section of this passage and is presented as the example of total self-giving. In contrast to those who look for recognition and have their reward in the adulation and praise of men, this widow gives her all almost secretly. We are shown that the humble poor can make worthy offerings. In answer to the question 'Who is Jesus?' we are given an icon of a poor woman giving everything to the work of God.

- **Why does the Church still need to make a show of wealth and privilege? What sort of message does this carry to a world increasingly concerned with the starving?**

- **Are we obsessed with a person's clothing, background and education rather than their ability to present us with truthful answers?**

- **Is Mark guilty of a blanket condemnation of the scribes? Would he make a sweeping judgement of certain sections of the Church today?**

- **Is this picture of a poor widow one that speaks of Jesus and his mission?**

37

The Destruction of the Temple
Heralds the Beginning of Sorrows

Mark 13.1–13

¹**As he was leaving the temple, one of his** disciples said to him, "Look, Teacher! What massive stones! What magnificent buildings!" ²"Do you see all these great buildings?" replied Jesus. "Not one stone here will be left on another; every one will be thrown down." ³As Jesus was sitting on the Mount of Olives opposite the temple, Peter, James, John and Andrew asked him privately, ⁴"Tell us, when will these things happen? And what will be the sign that they are all about to be fulfilled?" ⁵Jesus said to them: "Watch out that no-one deceives you. ⁶Many will come in my name, claiming, 'I am he,' and will deceive many. ⁷When you hear of wars and rumours of wars, do not be alarmed. Such things must happen, but the end is still to come. ⁸Nation will rise against nation, and kingdom against kingdom. There will be earthquakes in various places, and famines. These are the beginning of birth-pains. ⁹"You must be on your guard. You will be handed over to the local councils and flogged in the synagogues. On account of me you will stand before governors and kings as witnesses to them. ¹⁰And the gospel must first be preached to all nations. ¹¹Whenever you are arrested and brought to trial, do not worry beforehand about what to say. Just say whatever is given you at the time, for it is not you speaking, but the Holy Spirit. ¹²"Brother will betray brother to death, and a father his child. Children will rebel against their parents and have them put to death. ¹³All men will hate you because of me, but he who stands firm to the end will be saved.

This strange and rather gloomy chapter is often known as the 'Markan apocalypse' and yet it has little in common with what we might expect from apocalyptic writing. There is no weird imagery like that of Daniel or Revelation. The passage is not totally obsessed with the events of the end-time. The writer is more concerned to warn against panic, to point out that there will be a series of events but everything is in the control of God. The reader is not to be anxious – even the words he has to use in court will be supplied by the Holy Spirit (v11). All that is required of the good disciple is to stand firm to the end (v13). The passage reiterates the basic Markan theme that discipleship involves suffering. Those who follow Jesus will be vindicated, but those who have stubbornly refused to respond to Jesus' teaching will be punished.

The chapter begins with the disciples overawed by the magnificence of the Temple. Even today the Temple in its wreckage still induces a similar response. Vast enormous stones witness to its former glory. In Jesus' time, when the Temple was newly built, the sight must have been awesome. For him to have foretold its destruction (v2) must have been breathtaking. Mark has Jesus following in the tradition of Jeremiah by embarking on a detailed prophecy which is echoed in John 2.19 and was referred to at his trial (Mark 14.57; 15.29; Matt. 26.59–61; 27.40). The fate of the Temple is inevitably linked with that of the city of Jerusalem which was destroyed by the Romans in AD 70. The discourse moves from the Temple to the 'end' of all things and warns the disciples of what must be endured. Above all, the disciple must be on guard (v5, 9). These 'birth-pains' (v8) will bring about a new beginning. These disasters are a necessary prelude to the 'end' which is not yet (v7).

- **Was it necessary for the Temple worship to be swept away?**

- **Does this suggest that a Church over-concerned with ritual and correct ceremonial is in danger?**

- **Are we easily impressed by awesome buildings?**

- **Can we recognize 'birth-pains' in our own day?**

- **Why is the 'end' still being delayed? Is it because the Gentile mission is still incomplete (v10)?**

- **Can we accept the link between discipleship and suffering?**

38

The Disastrous Abomination
and the Son of Man

Mark 13.14–27

[14]"**When you see 'the abomination that causes desolation'** standing where it does not belong - let the reader understand - then let those who are in Judea flee to the mountains. [15]Let no-one on the roof of his house go down or enter the house to take anything out. [16]Let no-one in the field go back to get his cloak. [17]How dreadful it will be in those days for pregnant women and nursing mothers! [18]Pray that this will not take place in winter, [19]because those will be days of distress unequalled from the beginning, when God created the world, until now - and never to be equalled again. [20]If the Lord had not cut short those days, no-one would survive. But for the sake of the elect, whom he has chosen, he has shortened them. [21]At that time if anyone says to you,

'Look, here is the Christ!' or, 'Look, there he is!' do not believe it. [22]For false Christs and false prophets will appear and perform signs and miracles to deceive the elect - if that were possible. [23]So be on your guard; I have told you everything ahead of time.

[24]"But in those days, following that distress,

"'the sun will be darkened, and the moon will not give its light;
[25]the stars will fall from the sky, and the heavenly bodies will be shaken.'

[26]"At that time men will see the Son of Man coming in clouds with great power and glory. [27]And he will send his angels and gather his elect from the four winds, from the ends of the earth to the ends of the heavens.

At last Jesus appears to answer the question the four disciples asked in v4. The destruction of the Temple (and Jerusalem with it) will occur when you see this sign, the abomination that causes desolation set up. What on earth is Jesus talking about? Mark is aware that Jesus is speaking in code, and indicates this with a strange editorial aside in v14 when you can almost hear him saying 'Psst! You know what this means!' Apocalyptic literature often resorted to cryptic codes and cultivated a climate of innuendo, the reason being that it was sometimes dangerous to speak too directly. The term 'abomination that causes desolation' was used in the apocalyptic book of Daniel (Dan. 12.11) to refer to the altar of Zeus which was set up in the Temple by the Hellenistic

Antiochus Epiphanes in 168 BC (compare 1 Macc. 1.54–9). Anything connected with idolatry was an 'abomination' and it appears that Jesus is expecting a similar desecration to occur. In fact the dreadful Emperor Caligula did threaten to set up a statue of himself as a god in the Temple in AD 40. This abomination did not take place, but Josephus tells us the soldiers of Titus set up their standards in the Temple and proclaimed him as a divine emperor in AD 70. This abomination triggered the destruction of the Temple and the sack of Jerusalem. The big issue for Mark's gospel is that this event signals the end for Judaism.

Jesus is warning that everyone should flee and be on guard against false Messiahs. The good news is that after these tumultuous events, when the whole of nature is shaken, the faithful elect will see the Son of Man 'coming in clouds with great power and glory' (v26) and the scattered elect will be gathered to him. This dramatic imagery, so dependent on Daniel 7, reinforces the idea in Mark 3.14 that the disciple's role is to 'be with Jesus' in suffering and in glory. Three of the four disciples who receive this apocalyptic answer have already glimpsed a vision of Jesus as the Son of Man at the transfiguration (9.2–13).

• **What abominations do we see in our present society? Are they idolatrous?**

• **Are they enough to spark a religious reaction?**

• **Why has not the Son of Man come to call his elect? Or has he?**

• **Can you relate this disaster (the fall of Jerusalem) to the many disasters in our own time?**

39

Look to the Fig Tree

Mark 13.28–37

²⁸"Now learn this lesson from the fig-tree: As soon as its twigs get tender and its leaves come out, you know that summer is near. ²⁹Even so, when you see these things happening, you know that it is near, right at the door. ³⁰I tell you the truth, this generation will certainly not pass away until all these things have happened. ³¹Heaven and earth will pass away, but my words will never pass away. ³²"No-one knows about that day or hour, not even the angels in heaven, nor the Son, but only the Father. ³³Be on guard! Be alert! You do not know when that time will come. ³⁴It's like a man going away: He leaves his house and puts his servants in charge, each with his assigned task, and tells the one at the door to keep watch.

³⁵"Therefore keep watch because you do not know when the owner of the house will come back - whether in the evening, or at midnight, or when the cock crows, or at dawn. ³⁶If he comes suddenly, do not let him find you sleeping. ³⁷What I say to you, I say to everyone: 'Watch!'"

Mark is again reflecting on the fig tree which was cursed not so long ago (11.14). Sadly, like Judaism, it had not come into fruit. In Judaism the fig tree was seen to be one of the first harbingers of summer and it was used to symbolize the joys of the messianic age. Sadly it seems as if the fig tree, so full of promise, has failed to deliver. Instead of a harvest we see disaster strike. The reason is the failure of Judaism to recognize its Messiah in Jesus. The disciples are to learn from this and to be consoled with the knowledge that although everything appears to be in flux, the words of Jesus will remain (v31).

The passage concludes with more warnings about remaining alert (v33). This is illustrated with a short parable about a servant remaining watchful for his master's return. Are we to conclude from this that the 'end' will come suddenly, like the master who returns from his journey without warning? Are we to see the passage as a development of the Church's longing for the return of Christ in the second coming?

Whatever we conclude, the emphasis is strongly centred on the need for vigilance. The disciple is repeatedly told to stay awake to be watchful and ready. We are reminded of the failure of Peter, James and John to live up to this request in the Garden of Gethsemane (14.32–42).

- Is one of the central requirements of a disciple to remain alert and watchful? Are we fulfilling this role?

- How often do we find ourselves dozing in an ecclesiastical stupor?

- How able are we to read the signs of the times? Is the prophetic tradition of perception still alive in our church?

- Is Mark being anti-Semitic here, or simply condemning all fruitless forms of religion and beliefs?

40

Evil Is Plotted and a Good Work Is Done

Mark 14.1–11

¹Now the Passover and the Feast of Unleavened Bread were only two days away, and the chief priests and the teachers of the law were looking for some sly way to arrest Jesus and kill him. ²"But not during the Feast," they said, "or the people may riot."
³While he was in Bethany, reclining at the table in the home of a man known as Simon the Leper, a woman came with an alabaster jar of very expensive perfume, made of pure nard. She broke the jar and poured the perfume on his head.
⁴Some of those present were saying indignantly to one another, "Why this waste of perfume? ⁵It could have been sold for more than a year's wages and the money given to the poor." And they rebuked her harshly.
⁶"Leave her alone," said Jesus. "Why are you bothering her? She has done a beautiful thing to me. ⁷The poor you will always have with you, and you can help them any time you want. But you will not always have me. ⁸She did what she could. She poured perfume on my body beforehand to prepare for my burial. ⁹I tell you the truth, wherever the gospel is preached throughout the world, what she has done will also be told, in memory of her."
¹⁰Then Judas Iscariot, one of the Twelve, went to the chief priests to betray Jesus to them. ¹¹They were delighted to hear this and promised to give him money. So he watched for an opportunity to hand him over.

We begin with a short paragraph which confirms what Mark has been at pains to demonstrate from chapter 3 – the determination of the authorities to destroy Jesus. According to Mark's dating (v1) the authorities are resolved to have Jesus removed (v1) but not during the festival (v2). However, Judas' treachery (vv10–11) alters the situation so that they resolve to take full advantage of this new opportunity.

Meanwhile Jesus is invited to a supper party at Bethany. The story of Jesus' anointing occurs several times in the Gospels, with variations. In Luke 7.36–50 the woman is described as a sinner and anoints Jesus' feet, not his head. Simon is not a leper but a Pharisee. The emphasis is on forgiveness, not waste as in this story. In John, the whole incident takes place in Bethany, not at Simon's house but in the home of Lazarus, and it is his sister Mary who anoints Jesus' feet. Surprisingly, Mary Magdalene is not mentioned in any of these accounts despite her identification in Christian art as the woman in the story.

It may be impossible to reconstruct the original event, but for Mark (and the other Evangelists) it is a significant story in which Jesus appears not to be offered the usual courtesies by his hosts, and a woman anoints him instead. This is not merely a story of embarrassment at a supper party. It is seen as a ritual anointing of Jesus as the Christ ('Christ' means 'anointed one'). The fact that Jesus is anointed as king by a woman is a further twist in this remarkable story about a Messiah who is unrecognized until after his resurrection. Here again we have another sign of who Jesus is. Sadly the dinner guests are unable to make sense of it and Judas seems determined to put a stop to it.

- **Does the fact that this story of the anointing has different versions disturb you? What are the various Evangelists trying to say?**

- **Have we been too blinkered like Simon and his friends? Are we unable to see the full significance of symbolic gestures such as this?**

- **Do we have any understanding or sympathy with the chief priests who found Jesus a threat to the status quo?**

- **What do you think was Judas' motive in betraying Jesus?**

SECTION 9

OPEN TO STRUGGLE

41

The Last Supper
and Its Preparations

Mark 14.12–25

[12]On the first day of the Feast of Unleavened Bread, when it was customary to sacrifice the Passover lamb, Jesus' disciples asked him, "Where do you want us to go and make preparations for you to eat the Passover?" [13]So he sent two of his disciples, telling them, "Go into the city, and a man carrying a jar of water will meet you. Follow him. [14]Say to the owner of the house he enters, 'The Teacher asks: Where is my guest room, where I may eat the Passover with my disciples?' [15]He will show you a large upper room, furnished and ready. Make preparations for us there." [16]The disciples left, went into the city and found things just as Jesus had told them. So they prepared the Passover.

[17]When evening came, Jesus arrived with the Twelve. [18]While they were reclining at the table eating, he said, "I tell you the truth, one of you will betray me - one who is eating with me." [19]They were saddened, and one by one they said to him, "Surely not I?" [20]"It is one of the Twelve," he replied, "one who dips bread into the bowl with me. [21]The Son of Man will go just as it is written about him. But woe to that man who betrays the Son of Man! It would be better for him if he had not been born."

[22]While they were eating, Jesus took bread, gave thanks and broke it, and gave it to his disciples, saying, "Take it; this is my body." [23]Then he took the cup, gave thanks and offered it to them, and they all drank from it. [24]"This is my blood of the covenant, which is poured out for many," he said to them. [25]"I tell you the truth, I will not drink again of the fruit of the vine until that day when I drink it anew in the kingdom of God."

Mark continues his attempts at dating (v12). The confusion this creates need not detain us (the lambs were actually sacrificed the day before). What is clear is that Mark believes the last supper to have been a Passover meal and the link with the great Passover themes of Exodus, liberation, and new beginnings is very significant. The detailed preparations suggest well-laid plans and remind us of the world of spy thrillers (men do not usually carry water in jars (v13) as women do). It was important for Jesus to celebrate this last meal undisturbed. Everything is 'prepared' (v16) for the greatest events in history to unfold.

When Jesus reclines with his disciples at table he immediately upsets the gathering by foretelling his betrayal by one of the assembled disciples (v18). Leonardo's famous fresco, *The Last Supper* provides most of us with a visual image of this moment of consternation. However, we do need to remember that the posture was not one of sitting but reclining on cushions. The remark that the betrayer is one who has dipped in the same dish as Jesus almost pinpoints the offender to be one of the chief guests who would be lying either to the left or right of Jesus who is acting as host. As ever in this Gospel, Jesus is fully aware of what is going on, and can accept this act of betrayal as part of an ongoing plan foretold in Scripture. It is therefore in accordance with God's plan (v21). Like John the Baptist, Jesus is to be handed over (v18) not by an enemy but by one of his closest associates. It is by this cruel act of betrayal that God achieves his purpose.

It is in the context of anxiety, suspicion and betrayal that Jesus institutes the last supper in which he speaks of the sharing of his body (Greek *soma*). The Aramaic underlying this word suggests 'self' or 'personality' rather than merely the physical body. Is Jesus bequeathing his disciples his mission, his 'attitude' as Paul describes it? (Phil. 2.5). If so, it is this mind of Christ which must be disseminated among his followers if the work of the gospel is to continue. In this self-offering (v24) Jesus reinstates the covenant relationship so that the disciples can continue the work of the kingdom after his death (v25).

- **How do we understand this passage? Can you see how the last supper has developed into the eucharist? Have we lost something? Have we gained too much?**

- **Is the behaviour of the disciples set in contrast to that of Jesus who will share his bread with sinners?**

- **If Jesus does not exclude Judas from this meal, why does the Church place restrictions on who can receive communion?**

42

Gethsemane

Mark 14.26–42

²⁶**When they had sung a hymn, they went** out to the Mount of Olives. ²⁷"You will all fall away," Jesus told them, "for it is written:

"'I will strike the shepherd, and the sheep will be scattered.' ²⁸But after I have risen, I will go ahead of you into Galilee."

²⁹Peter declared, "Even if all fall away, I will not."

³⁰"I tell you the truth," Jesus answered, "today - yes, tonight - before the cock crows twice you yourself will disown me three times."

³¹But Peter insisted emphatically, "Even if I have to die with you, I will never disown you." And all the others said the same.

³²They went to a place called Gethsemane, and Jesus said to his disciples, "Sit here while I pray." ³³He took Peter, James and John along with him, and he began to be deeply distressed and troubled. ³⁴"My soul is overwhelmed with sorrow to the point of death," he said to them. "Stay here and keep watch."

³⁵Going a little farther, he fell to the ground and prayed that if possible the hour might pass from him. ³⁶"Abba, Father," he said, "everything is possible for you. Take this cup from me. Yet not what I will, but what you will."

³⁷Then he returned to his disciples and found them sleeping. "Simon," he said to Peter, "are you asleep? Could you not keep watch for one hour? ³⁸Watch and pray so that you will not fall into temptation. The spirit is willing, but the body is weak."

³⁹Once more he went away and prayed the same thing. ⁴⁰When he came back, he again found them sleeping, because their eyes were heavy. They did not know what to say to him. ⁴¹Returning the third time, he said to them, "Are you still sleeping and resting? Enough! The hour has come. Look, the Son of Man is betrayed into the hands of sinners. ⁴²Rise! Let us go! Here comes my betrayer!"

Mark frames his account of the last supper with examples of disciples' failure and disloyalty. Here Jesus returns to the theme of their imminent betrayal. He has no expectation of them. They will all be scattered (v27). They will all lose their faith, especially Peter, who is quick to protest his fidelity (v31). Despite their protestations of constancy, Jesus is well aware of their fallibility. However frail their faith he demonstrates his belief in them by arranging to meet them in Galilee after the resurrection (v28). This is a positive pointer to 16.7 and suggests that, despite their failures, the disciples will be, in the words of Wesley's hymn, 'ransomed, healed, restored, forgiven'.

All this is particularly poignant in a Gospel which commands discipleship in terms of losing life to find it (8.35), and which invites followers of Jesus to share in his sufferings. Sadly the Twelve consistently fail to comprehend what this means. At a time when they need to demonstrate their faith they are unable to watch and pray even for one hour (v37).

Mark does not contain an account of the Lord's prayer, and yet phrases of that prayer permeate this passage. 'Abba, Father' is Jesus' preferred mode of address to God whose will must be done (v36). The disciples are unable to stay awake and Jesus is about to be delivered into evil forces (v41). While alluding to this central prayer of the Christian faith, Mark also presents a very human Jesus struggling with the prospect of imminent suffering and death. Was it Jesus' hope that his people would respond to his preaching and embrace the kingdom for which the Lord's prayer pleads? If so, this scene is tragically drawn, for even his closest companions have failed to respond to this call, and Jesus is dealing with what appears to be failure.

- **How often do we fail to understand the implications of discipleship?**

- **Is our faith more bluster than belief? What would happen if we were put to the test?**

- **How do we deal with failure?**

- **Is the Lord's prayer a *crie de coeur* for God to intervene and rescue us?**

43

Jesus is Arrested

Mark 14.43–52

⁴³Just as he was speaking, Judas, one of the Twelve, appeared. With him was a crowd armed with swords and clubs, sent from the chief priests, the teachers of the law, and the elders. ⁴⁴Now the betrayer had arranged a signal with them: "The one I kiss is the man; arrest him and lead him away under guard." ⁴⁵Going at once to Jesus, Judas said, "Rabbi!" and kissed him. ⁴⁶The men seized Jesus and arrested him. ⁴⁷Then one of those standing near drew his sword and struck the servant of the high priest, cutting off his ear. ⁴⁸"Am I leading a rebellion," said Jesus, "that you have come out with swords and clubs to capture me? ⁴⁹Every day I was with you, teaching in the temple courts, and you did not arrest me. But the Scriptures must be fulfilled." ⁵⁰Then everyone deserted him and fled.

⁵¹A young man, wearing nothing but a linen garment, was following Jesus. When they seized him, ⁵²he fled naked, leaving his garment behind.

Mark makes dramatic use of his favourite phrase, *'Kai euthus'*, 'and immediately', while he was still speaking (v43) it happens: Jesus is betrayed by one of his followers with a kiss. So familiar are we with this story that it is difficult for us to feel the full impact of the horror it represents. Jesus is seized (v46) at the instigation of one of his own. Earlier he had described his disciples as his new family, his 'mother and brothers' (3.34). It was his own physical family – his real mother and brothers – who had attempted to have Jesus arrested in 3.21 (the same Greek verb *'paradidomi'* is used). Now the seizure has been effected by a member of his new family, and the death is sealed with a kiss. Jesus gives the impression that although he is bound he is still in control of events, for all this is happening to fulfil the Scriptures (v49). There is some token of resistance evidenced in the story of the unfortunate high priest's servant and his ear, also attested in John 18.10–11. Whatever happened, the tragedy is compounded by the flight of the disciples who, only hours previously, had been protesting their undying loyalty (v31).

The last two verses of this passage only appear in Mark. Both Matthew and Luke ignore it, probably because it made little sense to them as it might to us. Who is this young man who follows Jesus when the disciples have all fled? Why does he run away naked leaving behind his linen cloth? The fact that another young man in a linen cloth announces the resurrection to the frightened women (16.5) might provide a clue. Maybe this young man is the author himself who nakedly follows the naked Christ to his death only to be commissioned with announcing his resurrection. This is a Gospel of discipleship and the author is attempting to put this into practice. Every baptized disciple is called to be united in Christ's death and resurrection. (Rom. 6.3–4). The reference to a linen cloth (Greek '*sindon*') is a link with the baptismal garment. It is the same *sindon* in which the dead Christ is wrapped. So this Gospel begins and ends with references to baptism and its implications.

- **Is there a danger that the family of God (the Church) is deserting Jesus?**

- **Is there anything in our spiritual life that amounts to a betrayal of the gospel?**

- **We may be baptized, but do we put our baptismal vows into effect?**

44

Jesus before the Sanhedrin

Mark 14.53–65

⁵³**They took Jesus to the high priest, and all** the chief priests, elders and teachers of the law came together. ⁵⁴Peter followed him at a distance, right into the courtyard of the high priest. There he sat with the guards and warmed himself at the fire. ⁵⁵The chief priests and the whole Sanhedrin were looking for evidence against Jesus so that they could put him to death, but they did not find any. ⁵⁶Many testified falsely against him, but their statements did not agree. ⁵⁷Then some stood up and gave this false testimony against him. ⁵⁸"We heard him say, 'I will destroy this man-made temple and in three days will build another, not made by man.'" ⁵⁹Yet even then their testimony did not agree. ⁶⁰Then the high priest stood up before them and asked Jesus, "Are you not going to answer? What is this testimony that these men are bringing against you?" ⁶¹But Jesus remained silent and gave no answer.

Again the high priest asked him, "Are you the Christ, the Son of the Blessed One?"

⁶²"I am," said Jesus. "And you will see the Son of Man sitting at the right hand of the Mighty One and coming on the clouds of heaven." ⁶³The high priest tore his clothes. "Why do we need any more witnesses?" he asked. ⁶⁴"You have heard the blasphemy. What do you think?"

They all condemned him as worthy of death. ⁶⁵Then some began to spit at him; they blindfolded him, struck him with their fists, and said, "Prophesy!" And the guards took him and beat him.

Commentators from the time of Luke have had difficulty with this account of Jesus appearing before the Sanhedrin at midnight. Luke's solution is to drop Mark's version and tell of an early morning assembly. His concern is for plausibility. It is highly unlikely that the Sanhedrin would gather in the middle of the night to convene a charge against Jesus, so he presents the incident as a hearing rather than a trial. Mark's purpose is to present Jesus as being condemned by the Jewish authorities. Even though they appear not to have power to impose the death penalty, they are fully implicated in bringing the accusation that will result in the crucifixion of Jesus on a trumped-up political charge.

We have to recognize that because of strained relations between Jews and Christians at the time of writing, the Evangelists may have exaggerated Jewish responsibility. Indeed it was only recently that the Church apologized to the Jewish community for accusing them of deicide. The Evangelists will be keen to play down Roman responsibility if they want to evangelize Gentiles.

Mark presents this material in his favourite 'sandwich' form. The account of the trial is wrapped around the denial of Peter, which only serves to emphasize the isolation of Jesus. A panel by the fourteenth-century Sienese painter, Duccio, makes the link between these two scenes by means of a staircase. Peter is below denying he ever knew Jesus while Jesus is being quizzed above on the very words that Peter confessed at Caesarea Philippi (8.29). This Gospel is written to answer precisely the question that the High Priest asks (remember the opening verse, 1.1). Ironically it is the high priest who (unknowingly) proclaims who Jesus really is. Jesus merely replies 'I am' (Greek *'ego eimi'*).

Jesus is also accused of threatening to destroy the Temple (v58). He was merely warning of its destruction which will now be inevitable. By rejecting Jesus, the nation brings down judgement on itself. In tearing his robe, the high priest prefigures the tearing of the Temple veil (15.38). The whole passage is heavy with Markan irony.

- **Is the New Testament anti-Semitic? Is there an over-exaggeration here that we need to guard against or even apologize for?**
- **What does it mean to confess Jesus as 'the Christ, the Son of the Blessed One'?**
- **Why does Jesus prefer to talk in terms of a 'Son of Man' rather than a 'Son of God'?**
- **Was Jesus guilty of blasphemy?**

45

Peter Denies He Knew Jesus

Mark 14.66–72

⁶⁶**While Peter was below in the courtyard,** one of the servant girls of the high priest came by. ⁶⁷When she saw Peter warming himself, she looked closely at him.

"You also were with that Nazarene, Jesus," she said.

⁶⁸But he denied it. "I don't know or understand what you're talking about," he said, and went out into the entrance.

⁶⁹When the servant girl saw him there, she said again to those standing around, "This fellow is one of them." ⁷⁰Again he denied it.

After a little while, those standing near said to Peter, "Surely you are one of them, for you are a Galilean."

⁷¹He began to call down curses on himself, and he swore to them, "I don't know this man you're talking about."

⁷²Immediately the cock crowed the second time. Then Peter remembered the word Jesus had spoken to him: "Before the cock crows twice you will disown me three times." And he broke down and wept.

For a Gospel which hinges on discipleship as a confession of faith in Jesus, this is a devastating passage. Here we have the spokesman of the Twelve, the one who first confessed Jesus as the Christ, now openly denying he ever knew him. The irony is compounded when, with the flourish of a storyteller, Mark tells us that Peter, the chief disciple, denies Jesus, not once but three times. All this while the high priest is questioning Jesus about his messianic status. Had the disciples the faith to pray not to be led into the time of trial ('temptation' v38), then maybe this might not have happened. As it is, Peter has failed miserably to follow Jesus, which was his original commission ('follow me' 1.16). Discipleship is no easy option and the readers of this Gospel are reminded that if they are to 'drink the cup that Jesus drinks and be baptised with the baptism he is baptised with' (10.38), this will involve standing firm when the going gets tough. Peter is fulfilling Jesus' prophecy made at the time of his confession, that there will be some who will be ashamed to be known as followers of Jesus (8.38). Indeed

Jesus himself had foretold that this would happen (14.30). 'Immediately' (*'Kai euthus'*) – Mark's characteristic phrase is employed with dramatic effect to remind us that Jesus' prophecy is fulfilled (v72). 'Before the cock crows twice you yourself will disown me three times.' It is little wonder that Peter 'broke down and wept'. The Greek suggests he throws himself down – a dejected figure who can only be raised up by the risen Christ. We are reminded of the words of Jack Winslow's hymn:

> Lord of all power
> Lord of all being, I give you my all;
> if e'er I disown you I stumble and fall.

- Can we confess to being ashamed of our faith when put to the test? Do we feel intellectually disadvantaged, slightly ridiculous or even irrelevant when thought of as Christians?

- How do we cope with hostile accusatory questions about our faith? Is there a way to witness to our belief in Jesus when being slandered?

- Do we, like Peter, lose our temper when put under pressure? Notice how once a lie is told the web of deceit is compounded.

- How do we cope with being found out and recognizing our failure?

SECTION 10

OPEN TO DEATH
AND RESURRECTION

46

Jesus before Pilate

Mark 15.1–15

¹**Very early in the morning, the chief priests,** with the elders, the teachers of the law and the whole Sanhedrin, reached a decision. They bound Jesus, led him away and turned him over to Pilate.

²"Are you the king of the Jews?" asked Pilate. "Yes, it is as you say," Jesus replied.

³The chief priests accused him of many things. ⁴So again Pilate asked him, "Aren't you going to answer? See how many things they are accusing you of."

⁵But Jesus still made no reply, and Pilate was amazed.

⁶Now it was the custom at the Feast to release a prisoner whom the people requested. ⁷A man called Barabbas was in prison with the insurrectionists who had committed murder in the uprising. ⁸The crowd came up and asked Pilate to do for them what he usually did.

⁹"Do you want me to release to you the king of the Jews?" asked Pilate, ¹⁰knowing it was out of envy that the chief priests had handed Jesus over to him. ¹¹But the chief priests stirred up the crowd to have Pilate release Barabbas instead.

¹²"What shall I do, then, with the one you call the king of the Jews?" Pilate asked them.

¹³"Crucify him!" they shouted.

¹⁴"Why? What crime has he committed?" asked Pilate.

But they shouted all the louder, "Crucify him!" ¹⁵Wanting to satisfy the crowd, Pilate released Barabbas to them. He had Jesus flogged, and handed him over to be crucified.

Events move at a fast pace (v1). Jesus is 'turned over' to the emperor's representative, Pontius Pilate. Pilate was procurator or more correctly 'prefect' of the province (an inscription describing him as such can be seen in Caesarea, the Roman capital of Judea). As such he is responsible for law and order and is likely to be resident in Jerusalem at politically sensitive times such as Passover. The way the Gospels portray Pilate as oscillating, indecisive and eager to please the crowds hardly fits the contemporary descriptions of him by Philo and Josephus who refer to him as 'inflexible, merciless and cruel'. Mark's presentation is of a man who merely carries out a sentence already pronounced by the Sanhedrin.

We have to recognize that this presentation is part of the process of shifting blame for the death of Jesus on to the Jewish authorities. We are told here that they make the accusations, they stir up the crowd and they demand the death penalty. In contrast to all this Pilate strives to release Jesus (vv5–14) and declares him harmless (v14). It has to be admitted that there is no record of a Passover prisoner being freed.

All this suggests that the Evangelist may not know exactly what happened at the trial. What is presented here is a reconstruction more concerned with blaming the Jewish authorities and whitewashing Roman responsibility. Verse 2 is witness to the fact that Jesus is presented on a political charge. 'Are you the King of the Jews?' As in the trial before the high priest, the claim is made not by Jesus but by his accuser (14.61). By showing him as remaining silent, Mark portrays Jesus as a dignified figure who has been reluctant during his life to acknowledge such claims. Now he will die with this claim nailed over his head. Although Pilate is 'amazed' at Jesus (v5) he is unable to control events, and, despite vain attempts to appease the crowd, he has Jesus savagely flogged and 'handed him over to be crucified' (v15).

- Mark's use of the verb 'to hand over' (Greek *'paradidomi'*) suggests Jesus is being treated like some sort of parcel. Do you think he is a willing victim or is he caught up in an inevitable course of events?

- If this account is an imaginative reconstruction based more on Old Testament texts than known facts, does it mean we cannot fully trust Mark?

- Do we not have to admit that imaginative reconstructions were the preferred literary device to convey a believed truth? (There are countless examples in ancient literature.)

- Can we distinguish between fact and truth? ('The English', said George Bernard Shaw, 'are unable to make such a distinction'!)

47

Jesus Is Mocked and Crucified

Mark 15.16–32

¹⁶The soldiers led Jesus away into the palace (that is, the Praetorium) and called together the whole company of soldiers. ¹⁷They put a purple robe on him, then twisted together a crown of thorns and set it on him. ¹⁸And they began to call out to him, "Hail, king of the Jews!" ¹⁹Again and again they struck him on the head with a staff and spat on him. Falling on their knees, they paid homage to him. ²⁰And when they had mocked him, they took off the purple robe and put his own clothes on him. Then they led him out to crucify him. ²¹A certain man from Cyrene, Simon, the father of Alexander and Rufus, was passing by on his way in from the country, and they forced him to carry the cross. ²²They brought Jesus to the place called Golgotha (which means The Place of the Skull). ²³Then they offered him wine mixed with myrrh, but he did not take it. ²⁴And they crucified him. Dividing up his clothes, they cast lots to see what each would get.

²⁵It was the third hour when they crucified him. ²⁶The written notice of the charge against him read: THE KING OF THE JEWS. ²⁷They crucified two robbers with him, one on his right and one on his left, ²⁸[and the scripture was fulfilled which says, "He was counted with the lawless ones".] ²⁹Those who passed by hurled insults at him, shaking their heads and saying, "So! You who are going to destroy the temple and build it in three days, ³⁰come down from the cross and save yourself!" ³¹In the same way the chief priests and the teachers of the law mocked him among themselves. "He saved others," they said, "but he can't save himself! ³²Let this Christ, this King of Israel, come down now from the cross, that we may see and believe." Those crucified with him also heaped insults on him.

As the three passion predictions foretold, Jesus is finally handed over (10.33) to be mocked (10.34) scourged and spat upon. Now that this is happening, Mark emphasizes the irony as well as the horror of these events by placing them next to the proclamation of Jesus as 'king of the Jews', words which are found on the lips of an incredulous Pilate (v9) and of the mocking soldiers (v18). The only crown this king will wear is made of thorns (v17). The only throne he will mount is a wooden cross. The mock homage they pay him is another example of Mark's theme throughout the passion narrative in which he portrays the enemies of Jesus as unwittingly proclaiming who he really is.

So, scourged and vilified, Jesus is led away to his death, a death which will proclaim his true identity. As Messiah and king he has been anointed, identified and proclaimed by people, most of whom have not understood their part in this great drama. The 'enthronement' continues in the most grisly circumstances of brutality and horror, suffering and anguish. For Mark the way to glory is by this road, this way of sorrows.

The reference to Simon of Cyrene being the father of Alexander and Rufus (v21) is found only in Mark, and they must have been familiar to Mark's readers. The fact that Simon was compelled to carry Jesus' cross is another irony when we remember the would-be disciple was invited to do so (8.34). Psalm 22 haunts this passage (sharing out his clothes, casting lots, see Ps. 22.18). The Evangelists were increasingly concerned to show that everything happened 'according to the Scriptures'. Further irony is compounded by the mention of a title over his head, 'King of the Jews'. Ironically it is two robbers who occupy the places sought by James and John in 10.37. The demands of the passers-by that he prove himself to be 'King of Israel' is the final twist.

- **How does the crucifixion demonstrate that Jesus is the Messiah?**
- **Is Jesus demonstrating the truth of his teaching that anyone who loses his life for the sake of the gospel will save it?**
- **Does the cross and its meaning reflect the reversal of values that Jesus represents to a world obsessed with the exercise of power and the pursuit of status?**
- **Can you see the crucifixion in terms of an enthronement?**

The Death of Jesus

Mark 15.33–39

³³At the sixth hour darkness came over the whole land until the ninth hour. ³⁴And at the ninth hour Jesus cried out in a loud voice, *"Eloi, Eloi, lama sabachthani?"* - which means, "My God, my God, why have you forsaken me?"

³⁵When some of those standing near heard this, they said, "Listen, he's calling Elijah." ³⁶One man ran, filled a sponge with wine vinegar, put it on a stick, and offered it to Jesus to drink. "Now leave him alone. Let's see if Elijah comes to take him down," he said. ³⁷With a loud cry, Jesus breathed his last. ³⁸The curtain of the temple was torn in two from top to bottom. ³⁹And when the centurion, who stood there in front of Jesus, heard his cry and saw how he died, he said, "Surely this man was the Son of God!"

Unlike the other Evangelists, Mark's presentation of the death of Jesus is characterized by utter desolation. Jesus is deserted and betrayed by his followers who have failed to understand the meaning of discipleship in terms of suffering and sacrifice. He is despised and rejected by the Jewish authorities, the crowds have deserted him and now mock him. He is 'woefully arrayed', nailed naked to a tree and feels himself forsaken by God himself. Hence the harrowing cry of dereliction in v34.

So for Mark (and Matthew who follows him) Jesus dies totally at one with the agony of the human condition. His cry is the scream of the human race which feels itself adrift in a sea of chaos battered by the storms of life. The fact that much of this material is influenced by Psalm 22 only serves to underscore the fact that the psalmist too was trying to express human despair in terms of being deserted by God.

These terrible events are reflected in the climatic conditions – 'darkness came over the whole land'. It is as though a pall of horror has fallen over the dreadful scene – now that Israel has finally rejected its king. The fact that we have difficulty in accepting a picture of Jesus dying in despair is nothing new. Both Luke and John omit this cry of desolation.

The mention of Elijah (v35) is a reminder that he was expected at the time of Messiah's appearing. He was also expected to intervene to rescue the righteous man from his suffering.

Jesus dies uttering a loud inarticulate cry (v37) which results in the exposure of the Holy of Holies in the Temple (v38). Is this another irony? The true nature of God has been revealed for those with eyes to see. One who does see is Jesus' executioner. The centurion makes the amazing confession that 'this man was the Son of God!' (v39), the same form of words used at the beginning of this Gospel. Whether or not the centurion is aware of the full meaning of his words does not matter – a representative of the Roman Empire has confessed who Jesus is. Many more will follow his example as the good news spreads.

- **Does it help or hinder our understanding of Jesus to see him die in despair?**

- **Have we become anaesthetized to the horror of these events?**

- **Why was it necessary for Jesus to be 'obedient to death – even death on a cross'**

49

The Burial of Jesus

Mark 15.40–47

⁴⁰**Some women were watching from a** distance. Among them were Mary Magdalene, Mary the mother of James the younger and of Joses, and Salome. ⁴¹In Galilee these women had followed him and cared for his needs. Many other women who had come up with him to Jerusalem were also there. ⁴²It was Preparation Day (that is, the day before the Sabbath). So as evening approached, ⁴³Joseph of Arimathea, a prominent member of the Council, who was himself waiting for the kingdom of God, went boldly to Pilate and asked for Jesus' body. ⁴⁴Pilate was surprised to hear that he was already dead. Summoning the centurion, he asked him if Jesus had already died. ⁴⁵When he learned from the centurion that it was so, he gave the body to Joseph. ⁴⁶So Joseph bought some linen cloth, took down the body, wrapped it in the linen, and placed it in a tomb cut out of rock. Then he rolled a stone against the entrance of the tomb. ⁴⁷Mary Magdalene and Mary the mother of Joses saw where he was laid.

If the disciples had all fled, the women at least kept a watch, albeit from a discreet distance (v40). At least they were fulfilling some of the expectations of discipleship, to 'watch' and presumably 'pray'. The identity of these women is not too clear and Matthew, who follows Mark closely here, makes some variations. Their purpose is to pave the way for their reappearance at the resurrection, suggesting that those who see and understand these events, even at a distance, will be able to receive the good news of the resurrection. Mark mentions a company of women present, 'who had come with [Jesus] up to Jerusalem' (v41). Luke mentions a similar company of women who provide for Jesus.

Other help is provided in the form of Joseph of Arimathea (v43) – obviously a man of substance and influence 'who was himself waiting for the kingdom of God'. Deuteronomy 21.23 demanded that a malefactor's body be removed from the tree before sundown. The burial is an act of compassion and was also in accordance with the Jewish law.

Pilate is said to have given permission and the burial is effected. Jesus is wrapped in a shroud (*'sindon'* the same Greek word that we came across in 14.52), and is buried without the customary embalming, presumably because of the lack of time as the Sabbath was about to start.

Jesus is buried in accordance with the law by a stranger who may or may not have been sympathetic to his cause. The women who witness the death also 'saw where he was laid' (v47).

- **What does the phrase 'waiting for the kingdom of God' mean?**

- **Is this another example of Markan irony – a man looking for the kingdom of God unknowingly lays the body of its proclaimer in a tomb?**

- **If this is a Gospel about discipleship and the identity of Jesus, where are the disciples when the true nature of the master is revealed?**

- **Is it the case that women are more reflective and perceptive than men at such times?**

50

The Empty Tomb
and the Challenge to Begin Again

Mark 16.1–8

¹**When the Sabbath was over, Mary** Magdalene, Mary the mother of James, and Salome bought spices so that they might go to anoint Jesus' body. ²Very early on the first day of the week, just after sunrise, they were on their way to the tomb ³and they asked each other, "Who will roll the stone away from the entrance of the tomb?"

⁴But when they looked up, they saw that the stone, which was very large, had been rolled away. ⁵As they entered the tomb, they saw a young man dressed in a white robe sitting on the right side, and they were alarmed. ⁶"Don't be alarmed," he said. "You are looking for Jesus the Nazarene, who was crucified. He has risen! He is not here. See the place where they laid him. ⁷But go, tell his disciples and Peter, 'He is going ahead of you into Galilee. There you will see him, just as he told you.'"

⁸Trembling and bewildered, the women went out and fled from the tomb. They said nothing to anyone, because they were afraid.

These last eight verses of the Gospel constitute the original ending of Mark. All that follows (vv9–20) are unknown to Matthew and Luke and appear to be a summary of their material. The language and vocabulary show signs of a later addition, possibly as late as the second century. Did Mark intend to finish his Gospel in mid sentence? (The last word in Greek is a preposition *'gar'*). Did he intend to write more, or is this the final draft?

We cannot be absolutely sure, but most scholars agree that v8 is the final verse and Mark ends his Gospel on a note of fear. There is certainly no textual evidence for any other ending.

In common with the other Evangelists, the actual resurrection is not described. We simply have an account of women coming to the tomb to anoint the body at the first opportunity early on the Sunday morning. The women are mentioned by name yet again, but with some inconsistencies. They bring spices to anoint the body, not an enviable task thirty-six hours after death. They are too late, for the body is not there. Besides which, Jesus' body had already been anointed for his burial by another woman in Mark 14.3–9.

They are surprised to find the stone rolled away from the tomb, and a young man dressed in a white robe – the dress of the newly baptized – announces that Jesus is not here but is raised from the dead. He then commissions the women to proclaim the good news to the disciples, and Peter in particular for Jesus has gone ahead to Galilee where he will meet them. This announcement causes amazement among the women. They had no expectation of a resurrection. They had no hope of seeing Jesus alive again. The young man is in effect inviting them and the disciples to follow Jesus again for 'he is going ahead of you'. In other words they, and Peter especially, are forgiven for their failures in discipleship and are being invited to a fresh start in Galilee – the place where they were originally called. Had the Gospel ended here at v7, we would have a happy ending full of hope and new beginnings. But v8 tells us the women were too frightened to convey the good news for they were 'afraid'. Mark's final irony is to point out that men and women have consistently failed to understand and act on the truth as it is laid out before them. They are paralysed by fear.

- Obviously someone must have conveyed something of the good news for Mark to be able to write his story. Is this cynicism justified? Are we still disobediently remaining silent for fear of the consequences of following Jesus who has gone before us?

- How closely is forgiveness and renewal associated with a fresh start? Are we ready to be true disciples in this Markan sense?

- Is this Gospel a baptism treatise – a final call to renounce self, take up the cross and follow Christ? Mark begins and ends with allusions to baptism and its theology.

Appendix I

An Interview with Mark,
the writer of this Gospel

I have often been fascinated by the author of this Gospel, and longed to meet him and ask a few questions about his Gospel and how he came to write it. Of course I shall have to wait until the next life for such an opportunity, but somehow within what the Church calls the communion of the saints it should be permissible to speculate on some of his answers.

Me: Your work has often been described as a 'passion narrative with an introduction'. Do you think this is a fair description?

Mark: It may be. I prefer to think of it as a proclamation, a statement of faith for those about to be baptized.

Me: So your work is related to baptism. Is that why you chose to begin with the baptism of Jesus rather than his birth or genealogy?

Mark: My gospel is about the Christian life and how to live it as a follower of Jesus. Information about his birth is irrelevant to that. How does it help my purpose to tell you stories about shepherds and wise men? Others have found that useful to their purpose – it forms no part of my story on discipleship.

Me: Your mention of discipleship reminds me of the poor treatment you gave Peter and the 'Twelve'. Do you think you've been harsh on them, painting them as obdurate, stupid and short-sighted?

Mark: All they lacked was faith. Had they the faith of a grain of mustard seed then mountains would have moved for them. Jesus exhausted himself in trying to build up their faith – the faith we all confess at baptism.

Me: How do you define a disciple?

Mark: A disciple is someone who is 'with Jesus'. That is, someone who has the heart and mind of Jesus – his outlook and attitude on life – or, as Paul would say, someone incorporated into Christ as part of his body. John too makes the same point: the disciples are to be united in Christ as branches of the vine.

Whether they are living stones, parts of the body or branches of the vine, disciples must be with Jesus – part of his new family. The great danger for the Church both then and now is that so-called disciples soon fall away like some of the seed in the parable of the sower.

Me: Do you think the Church today has a better understanding of what you mean by discipleship?

Mark: No. The Church today is no better than the disciples who, protesting their loyalty to Christ, forsook him and fled. Maybe some of your women are more responsive. Like the women in my Gospel they are more ready to see an opportunity. However, they too stand at a distance noting the demise of the Church and its inability to unite itself to the gospel message, they too are sometimes paralysed by fear.

Me: If your Gospel is a proclamation of faith, then the amount of space you dedicate to the problem of suffering (in the passion predictions and the passion narrative) suggests that you see the good news as related to pain and persecution.

Mark: Jesus came to proclaim the kingdom of God. When that happens, the forces of evil align their opposition. My gospel is about conflict. It is a conflict between truth and ignorance, between God's rule and the forces of darkness. The final conflict is played out in the story of the passion. Many of my first readers were undergoing fierce persecution for their beliefs and understood what this means.

Me: Did you come across your material in any connected form, or are you responsible for your own presentation?

Mark: Some of what I deliver was recounted to me in a connected form. The story of the passion is a story with a beginning and an end. Followers of Jesus would tell this tale to each other and I edited it for my own purposes, including material that would illuminate some of the story. The story of the fig tree, for example, has a lot to say about the Jewish rejection of Jesus and its consequences, and similarly the story of the wicked husbandmen. Other stories or sermons would be connected by a theme like a group of conflict stories, or parables, or miracle tales, or sayings on a theme. They get linked in the oral tradition, as your stories do. Your habit of telling jokes in a pub, for instance, where one joke will be followed by another person telling a similar joke. The stories about Jesus were circulated like that, often with a punchline rather like a joke has.

Me: Are you suggesting there is some humour in your work?

Mark: Of course, black humour, irony, even a little cynicism. For example, it takes a sense of humour for Simon, shaky and vacillating as he is, to be called a 'rock'. There is a mix of anger and humour that makes for a more human presentation of Jesus than you might be expecting.

Me: I notice your presentation of Jesus is much gruffer and more fierce than say that of Luke.

Mark: All of us Evangelists view Jesus from different perspectives. We are like Impressionist painters, we try to capture the vividness of what we see in the *'plein air'*. Or perhaps we are like students in a life class trying to re-create the model from a variety of viewpoints in a mixture of media. Perhaps I am a little more stark and graphic in my presentation.

Me: What is stark about your work is the ending. To finish on a note of fear and failure hardly merits the title 'good news', does it?

Mark: Yes, I have often been criticized for the abrupt ending. Indeed Matthew and Luke did not like it and added material of their own. Luke rather too much for my liking: writing a second volume in which the disciples sound almost too good to be true! However, despite a stupid second-century scribe trying to harmonize my work with that of everyone else, it seems at last the true ending is being recognized even if it is embarrassing.

Me: So you meant it to be uncomfortable and disturbing?

Mark: Of course! There is nothing comfortable or complacent in Christianity as I had to proclaim it. The message of Jesus was almost lost because of stupid disciples, an unresponsive nation and hostile authorities both religious and secular. Even his own family were against him. All he wanted was to fulfil the Father's will. He was driven by God's Spirit to proclaim the kingdom.

That kingdom would have been established had the disciples and the nation responded. But no, we were all either out to get him or determined to misunderstand him.

I have to include myself in this condemnation. The postscript I provide in the Garden of Gethsemane is a personal reference. I felt called to follow and was being prepared for baptism but when the going got tough I ran away naked. But I learnt something by being naked. I must forsake everything for the gospel. Take risks – be exposed – be as vulnerable as Jesus was when he was nailed, naked, to the cross. So I wrote my Gospel in an attempt to elicit a response from a Church which was failing Christ yet again.

Me: Why did the women run off, afraid to deliver their message?

Mark: Perhaps because they felt inadequate. Many women, even today, feel they are not up to this task. They are – they must respond even in the face of fierce opposition.

Me: Perhaps they ran off because they were terrified of what discipleship involves.

Mark: I am convinced the Church needs to rediscover the cost of discipleship as well as its rewards. The message is to take up your cross and follow the Son of Man who will be vindicated by God and his saints (Dan. 7). This chapter of Daniel haunts much of what I have to say. The Church today must recover its sense of community. Jesus needed his disciples to be 'with him'. The Son of Man was a corporate figure; in Daniel's vision he, together with the saints, receive the kingdom after a time of great suffering. This imagery stands behind much of what Jesus had to say in my Gospel. The victory over evil can only be secured if true discipleship is understood. The message we have to proclaim is one of a new community prepared to share in Jesus' baptism, drink his cup, and be united with him in establishing God's kingly rule. There is no need to be fearful. Turn around, repent and believe in this good news.

PALESTINE
in the time of JESUS

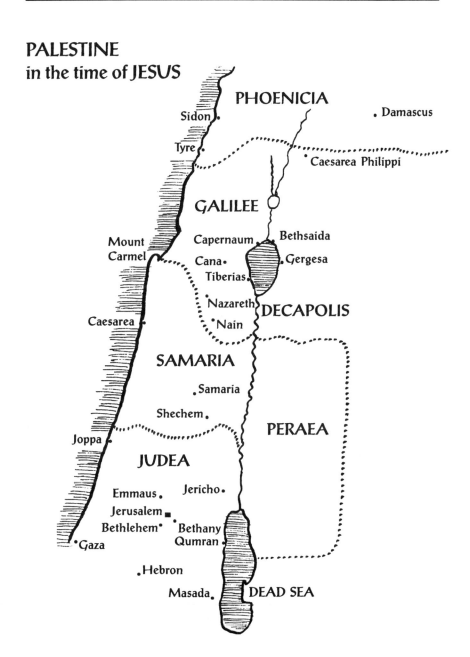

PHOENICIA

Sidon

. Damascus

Tyre

. Caesarea Philippi

GALILEE

Mount Carmel

Capernaum

Bethsaida

Cana.

Gergesa

Tiberias.

Nazareth

DECAPOLIS

Caesarea

Nain

SAMARIA

. Samaria

Shechem.

PERAEA

Joppa

JUDEA

Emmaus.

Jericho.

Jerusalem

Bethlehem

Bethany

Qumran.

Gaza

.Hebron

Masada.

DEAD SEA